THE BEAUTY OF THE KING.

THE
BEAUTY OF THE KING

BY THE

REV. RICHARD NEWTON, D.D.

AUTHOR OF

"THE KING'S HIGHWAY," "BIBLE WARNINGS," ETC.

SOLID GROUND CHRISTIAN BOOKS
PORT ST LUCIE, FLORIDA USA

Solid Ground Christian Books
1682 SW Pancoast Street
Port St Lucie, FL 34987
205-587-4480
www.solid-ground-books.com
mike.sgcb@gmail.com

THE BEAUTY OF THE KING
Sermons for Children on the Riches of the Grace
and the Wonders of the Love of Christ

By Richard Newton (1813-1887)

First Solid Ground Edition April 2018

Taken from 19th century edition by James Nisbet & Co

Cover Design by Borgo Design, Tuscaloosa, Alabama

ISBN: 978-159925-3800

PREFACE.

WE sometimes see a bright jewel which has many smooth polished sides or surfaces. It is pleasant to take up such a jewel; turn it carefully over; look at its many surfaces, one after another, and notice the different views they present of the beauty shining out from that precious stone.

Now, the character and work of the Lord Jesus Christ, our blessed Saviour, may well be compared to such a jewel. There are very many sides to this jewel. And there is a wonderful variety in the rays of light and loveliness, that shine out from these different sides. No two of them are exactly alike. It is an interesting and profitable study to examine this jewel carefully, and see the amazing brightness and beauty that are hid in it, and are all the time shining out from it.

The aim of the present volume is to assist the

young in doing this. Their attention is here called to a few of the shining surfaces of this great Jewel. Jesus, in the riches of His grace and the wonders of His love, is the one theme of these sermons.

If the reading of them shall help any of his young friends, in their efforts to know Jesus more, to love and serve Him better, and, in so doing, to be happier and more useful, the writer will feel abundantly rewarded for his labour.

R. N.

CONTENTS.

CHAP.		PAGE
I.	THE KING IN HIS BEAUTY	3
II.	THE BEAUTY OF THE KING	27
III.	THE KING IN THE BEAUTY OF HIS KINGDOM	51
IV.	THE BEAUTY OF THE KING'S FAMILY	71
V.	THE BEAUTY OF THE KING'S WORK—THE RAISING OF LAZARUS	95
VI.	THE BEAUTY OF THE KING'S WORK—THE GENERAL RESURRECTION	117
VII.	THE BEAUTY OF THE KING'S LESSONS—THE LESSON OF TRUST	139
VIII.	THE BEAUTY OF THE KING'S LESSONS—THE LESSON OF GENTLENESS	163
IX.	THE BEAUTY OF THE KING'S TITLES—JESUS COMPARED TO A ROCK	187
X.	THE BEAUTY OF THE KING'S TITLES—JESUS THE BREAD OF LIFE	211

I.

THE KING IN HIS BEAUTY.

"THINE EYES SHALL SEE THE KING IN HIS BEAUTY."
Isaiah xxxiii. 17.

I.

THE KING IN HIS BEAUTY.

THE King here spoken of is Jesus. This promise refers to heaven. There will be many glorious things for us to see when we get to heaven. But the grandest, and the most beautiful of all, will be to see Jesus Himself. The Apostle Paul says that there "we shall see Him as He is." It must have been a blessed thing to have seen Jesus when He was on earth; but *that* was nothing compared to what it will be to see Him in heaven. When Jesus was here, in this world, we have no reason to suppose that He was remarkable for the beauty of His appearance. We are not told, indeed, by the good men who wrote His life in the Gospels, how He looked. The prophet Isaiah is the only one of the sacred writers who has given any particular account of His appearance "when Jesus was seen among men." And he speaks of Him as—"a man of sorrows, and acquainted with grief; with no form, nor comeliness, and with no beauty that we should desire Him" (Isaiah liii. 2, 3).

But it will be very different when we come to see Jesus in heaven. There will be wonderful beauty and glory about Him there. And those who love and serve

Him here, will see all this beauty and glory there. Jesus prayed for this very thing when He was here on earth. In the 17th chapter of St. John's Gospel, we have written out for us the great prayer which Jesus offered for His people, just before He went to be crucified. In the twenty-fourth verse of that chapter, we have these wonderful words—"Father, I will that they also whom Thou hast given me, be with me where I am; *that they may behold my glory,* which Thou hast given me." These words of Jesus, in His prayer, give us the best explanation we can have of the meaning of the prophet Isaiah, when he wrote the sweet promise contained in our present text, "Thine eyes shall see the King in His beauty." If you ask me to tell you what this promise means, I would answer the question by turning to these words of Jesus in His prayer—"Father, I will that they also whom Thou hast given me, be with me where I am; that they may behold my glory." The King spoken of in one of these passages is Jesus, who is speaking Himself in the other passage. The "*beauty*" that Isaiah speaks of is the same thing as the "*glory*" that Jesus prays about. Isaiah calls it "the King's beauty." Jesus calls it—"*My glory.*" Isaiah does not tell us where this beauty was to be seen; but Jesus tells us. He says it will be—"*where I am.*" And we know very well where Jesus is. Jesus is in heaven. And every one who loves Jesus can look up to Him, and say—

> "'Tis where *Thou* art is heaven to me,
> And heaven without Thee cannot be."

And so these words of Isaiah lead our thoughts up to heaven—" Thine eyes shall see the King in His beauty." We all hope to go to heaven when we die. If we really love and serve Jesus, we certainly *shall* go there. And so we should be interested in hearing of what we are to see when we get there. God has not told us much concerning heaven. We should try to understand all that He has told us. The Apostle Paul was taken to heaven before he died, and then came back again to earth. He saw "the King in His beauty" there; but he never told about it. He said he was not allowed to tell what he had seen (2 Cor. xii. 4).

And so we can only learn about heaven by studying what God has told us of it in His blessed Word. This passage in Isaiah is one of the places in which it is spoken of. "Thine eyes shall see the King in His beauty."

And when we come to think of the beauty, or glory, of Jesus in heaven, there are *three* things with which that glory will be connected, and which we must speak of, in order to understand this subject properly.

The first of these is—THE PLACE—*where Jesus will be, when we see Him in His beauty.*

We call this place *heaven*. In the Bible it is compared to different things. Sometimes it is spoken of as a *paradise*, or garden, full of all bright and beautiful things. When Adam and Eve were first created, you know that God put them in such a garden, or paradise. In that garden, we are told that God made to grow "every tree that was pleasant to the eye and good for food.'

And we know they would have been perfectly happy there, if they had only minded what God told them. But Satan got in there, in the form of a serpent, and tempted them to eat of the tree of which God had said they must not eat. And then they were driven out. In this way that Paradise was lost. But Jesus came to restore it to us. And heaven is compared to a garden, because it will be a place in some respects like the garden of Eden. It will be a "Paradise Restored." But it will be better than that first Paradise, because Satan will never be allowed to get into it to tempt us. And we shall never sin, and never be put out of it. Heaven is spoken of as a paradise in 2 Cor. xii. 2, 4, and Rev. ii. 7.

Sometimes heaven is spoken of in the Bible as "*a country.*" Paul calls it—"a better country, that is a heavenly" (Heb. xi. 16). The original word here means a Fatherland. Canaan, you know, was the land, or country, promised to the Jews. And while they were toiling in Egypt, or travelling through the wilderness, it was the thought of that blessed country, that promised land, that cheered and comforted them. That was a beautiful country. God called it "a land flowing with milk and honey;" He said it was—"a good land, a land of brooks of water, of fountains and depths that spring out of valleys and hills; a land of wheat, and barley, and vines, and fig-trees, and pomegranates; a land of oil olive, and honey; a land wherein they should eat bread without scarceness, and not lack anything in it: a land whose stones are iron, and out of whose hills they might dig brass" (Deut. viii. 7-9). And so the land of Canaan was one of God's types, or figures of heaven. And when we read in the Bible about the fertility and glory of that land, it should lead us to think of heaven, the place where Jesus is, and where "our eyes shall see the King in His beauty."

Sometimes heaven is spoken of in the Bible as a kingdom, where all is "righteousness, and peace, and joy in the Holy Ghost" (Rom. xiv. 17). Sometimes it is spoken of as *a temple*, in which all God's people shall worship, and serve Him day and night, without ever feeling weary (Rev. iii. 12, iv. 8). Sometimes it is spoken of as *a building, a house, or home*, in which all who love God will be brought together, as one great family; all knowing and loving one another, and perfectly happy in being with Jesus, where He is, and "seeing the King in His beauty." This is the way in which Jesus Himself spoke of heaven, when He said—"In my Father's *house* are many mansions; I go to prepare a place for you" (John xiv. 2).

But the fullest description we have in the Bible of heaven, the place where Jesus is, is when it is compared to *a city*. In one place it is called "a *continuing city*" (Heb. xiii. 14). In another place it is spoken of as—"*a city that hath foundations, whose builder and maker is God*" (Heb. xi. 10). But it is in the last two chapters of the Bible that we have the fullest description of heaven. And here it is represented as a city. But it is the most beautiful city that any eye has ever seen, or any ear has ever heard of, or any mind has ever thought of. Gold, and pearls, and precious stones, are the only materials employed in the building of this city. Earthly houses have those parts of them which only are seen finished off beautifully. The foundations, and those parts not seen, are made of very coarse, rough materials. But it is very different with the house, or city, which Jesus is preparing as our heavenly home—the place where we are to "see the King in His beauty." The very *foundations* of this city, even down to the lowest of them, are made of precious stones. Each of its gates is made out of one vast pearl. The walls and streets of the city are all made of pure gold. Only think of a city *paved* with gold; where the people *walk* on gold, and where the gold is as fine and transparent as glass, so that you can *see through* it. How poor and mean the grandest palaces of earthly kings become compared with this!

How much beauty there will be in such a place as this! We see a great many beautiful things in this world of ours. A day in spring is beautiful, when the leaves are bursting open, and the flowers are coming out, and the birds are singing, and the air is balmy, and the sun is bright;—yes, a day in spring *is* beautiful. The rising sun is beautiful, and so is the setting sun. A moonlight night is beautiful. Our world is full of beauty. And yet this world is only the prison-house, in which God keeps His disobedient children. But if God can afford to make His prison-house so beautiful, how much more beautiful must the palace be in which His Son is to reign as King; and where His own dear

THE KING IN HIS BEAUTY. 9

children are to live for ever ? When the Psalmist is speaking of this place he says—"the *perfection* of beauty" is there (Ps. l. 2). There is no perfection of beauty in this world. Here the ripest fruit has some speck in it. The sweetest rose has a thorn on the stem, or a worm at the heart of it. The brightest sky has a cloud upon its surface; and the sun itself has dark spots on its face. There is something to mar the beauty of all our brightest things in this world. But in that world,—that city,—that place where Jesus is—there will be nothing to mar the beauty that is seen everywhere. It will all be "the perfection of beauty."

A little girl was gazing up at the starry sky one clear night. She seemed to be very much occupied in thinking about something. Her mother said to her, "What are you thinking about, my dear ?"

"O mamma!" she said, "I was thinking if the *outside* of heaven is so beautiful, how *very* beautiful it must be *inside !*"

A very sweet thought, indeed, and one we may often consider ourselves, when we look up at the sky, on a clear, bright night, and see how it sparkles in its loveliness. *That* is the outside of heaven.

Sometimes when people are dying the heavenly land, where Jesus is, comes very near them, so that they can see it before they die.

THE LAND BEYOND THE MOUNTAINS.

A little boy lay dying. His father and mother were sitting on one side of his little bed, and the doctor was waiting and watching near. He had been silent for some time, and appeared to sleep. They thought he might pass away as he slept. But suddenly his blue eyes opened, wide and clear, and a sweet smile broke over his face. He looked upwards very earnestly, and then turning to his mother said—"Mother, what is that beautiful land that I see there, beyond the mountains?"

"I don't see any mountains, my dear," said the mother.

"Look there, mother dear," he said, pointing up. "They are very near now: so large and high; and the country beyond them seems so beautiful! The people are so happy; *and there are no sick children there.* Is that the heavenly land I see?"

"Yes, my child," his mother sobbed, "that is the heavenly land where Jesus dwells."

"O mother!—O father! don't be sorry for me; but come after me, to that beautiful land. Good-bye, mother dear, I'm going now; and Jesus has sent His angel to carry me over the mountains."

These were his last words. He died in his mother's arms. The angel carried him over the mountains to "see the King in His beauty." But he had caught a glimpse of its brightness before he went away. The *beauty of the place* is one of the things that will help to make up the glory, or beauty, that we shall see in Jesus when we go to heaven.

The second thing will be—THE COMPANY—*about Jesus when we see Him in His beauty.*

However beautiful the *place* may be, which is to be our heaven, we never could be satisfied with that alone. Jewelled walls, and pearly gates, and golden streets are all very well. They must be wondrously beautiful. But these, of themselves, could never make us happy. When we go to the house we live in, and which we call *home*, what is it that makes it feel so sweet and pleasant to us? It is not the walls of the building. It is not the furniture of the rooms—the tables, the chairs, the carpets on the floor, or the pictures that hang on the walls. It is not these things that make that place home to us; but it is the presence there of a dear father or mother, of brothers and sisters, of those whom we love, and who, we know, love us. And so it will be with heaven. The *place* will have something to do with the beauty we shall see, and the happiness we shall enjoy there; but the *company* will have much more to do with it.

And now let us talk a little about the company we shall meet in heaven. Who will make up this company? Well, to begin with, the angels will form a part of this company. We are told in the Bible that there will be in heaven—"*an innumerable company of angels*" (Heb. xii. 22). I never saw an angel. You never saw an angel. No doubt that any of us would feel frightened, if we should see one come into the room where we were. But we know, from what the Bible tells us, that the angels are very beautiful. They are always spoken of as clothed in white. They are sometimes spoken of as having wings, but not always. Sometimes they have appeared in the form of men, or women, but without any wings. We are not told how they looked; but we know that they must be very beautiful in their appearance. And to see such a beautiful place as heaven is, filled with such beautiful beings as angels are, must help to make heaven very beautiful.

But now, I think I hear one of you say—"Ah! yes; the angels, I dare say, are very beautiful. But then I don't know them; and they don't know me. I should be afraid of them. I don't think I could feel at home, or happy with them."

This is very natural. And if there were to be none but angels in the company of heaven, it would not feel very much like home to us. But then there will be others in heaven besides the angels. All the good people that we read about in the Bible will be there. Abraham will be there; and so will Joseph, and David, and Daniel, and Peter, and John, and Paul. And all the good people, who have died since, will be there too.

But then the company of heaven comes nearer to us even than this. I suppose there is not one person who will read these pages, but has some friend, or relation, in heaven. Have you lost a beloved father, or mother, or uncle, or aunt, who loved Jesus? You will find them in heaven. Have you lost a dear brother, or sister, old enough to love and serve Jesus? You will find them in heaven. Hear what an aged minister once said, on this very point.

HEAVEN.

"When I was a boy I used to think of heaven as a glorious golden city, with jewelled walls, and gates of pearl, with nobody in it but the angels, and they were all strangers to me. But after awhile my little brother died; then I thought of heaven as that great city, full of angels, with just one little fellow in it that I was acquainted with. He was the only one I knew there at that time. Then another brother died, and there were two in heaven that I knew. Then my acquaintance began to die, and the number of my friends in heaven grew larger all the time. But, it was not till one of my own little ones was taken that I began to feel that I had a personal interest in heaven. Then a second went, and a third, and a fourth; and so many of my friends and loved ones have gone there, that it seems as if I knew more in heaven than I know on earth. And *now*, when my thoughts turn to heaven, it is not the gold, and the jewels, and the pearls that I think of—but the loved ones there. It is not the *place*, so much as the *company*, that makes heaven seem beautiful."

Have any of us lost dear little baby brothers and sisters, too young to learn about Jesus here? We shall find them in heaven. Did you ever think of this, that there are more children in heaven than there are grown people? It is so. Do you ask me how I know it? I will tell you.

It is very well known that more than half of the people born into this world die while they are children. *But Jesus takes all the little ones to heaven.* He taught us this Himself when He took them in His arms, put His hands on them, and blessed them; saying—" Suffer the little children to come unto me, and forbid them not; *for of such is the kingdom of heaven."*

Here, then, we are sure that at least one half of those born into the world go to heaven, because they die as children. But what becomes of the other half! Do they *all* go to heaven! Alas! No. A good many of them never love, or serve, or trust in Jesus. It is a sad thing to say it, but it is true, *they cannot go to heaven.* And if the whole of one half of those born into the world die as children, and thus go to heaven, and only part of the other half, who grow up to be men and women go to heaven, then it is plain, that as the whole of one half is greater than a part of the other half, there must be more children in heaven than there are grown people.

And some people think that when children die, and go to heaven, they do not grow up to be men and women, but that they always remain children. I am not able to say, for certain, that this is so; because God has not told us about it; and no one can tell us for Him. But I hope it may be so. For I do love children so much that I should like to think that *there will always be children in heaven*. But if they all grow up to be men and women, by and by, there will be no children there, and this, it seems to me, would not be so pleasant.

If you go into a garden you never find all the flowers in full bloom at the same time. Instead of this you will find, mingled with the full-blown flowers, some buds half opened, and others just beginning to open. And this variety adds very much to the beauty of the garden. But heaven is God's garden. Christian men and women will be the full-blown flowers in that garden; *and children will be the buds*. And it seems to me there will always be buds there, as well as flowers in full bloom. But God is much wiser than we are, *and whichever way He orders it will be the best.*

But this company in heaven will be all good, and kind, and holy. They will be all "made perfect." Here, in this world, we have no perfect children, and no perfect men and women. But we shall *all be perfect there.* There will be none blind, or deaf, or lame, or sick in heaven. There will be none cross, or proud, or selfish in heaven. There will be no ugliness of any kind in heaven. There will be perfect beauty in the place, and perfect beauty in the company there. And they will all know and love one another there. No one will feel a stranger, or alone in heaven.

It is a very painful feeling that we have when we find ourselves alone, and unknown, among strangers.

THE STRANGER NOT A STRANGER.

In the early settlement of the city of Cincinnati, there was only one way for persons to get there, and that was by means of the flat-boats that passed up and down the Ohio river.

On one occasion a boat landed there. It had come down the river from Pittsburgh. There was a company of people on board that boat, who were going to Cincinnati to live there. Their friends were expecting their arrival, and had met, down by the side of the river, to welcome them. As they left the boat their friends gathered around them, to shake hands with them, and give them the warmest kind of a welcome.

But in that company, who had just arrived, there was one who was a stranger. He had no friends, or any one that knew him in Cincinnati. There was no one there to shake hands with him, or bid him welcome to the place. He had been feeling lonely before, he felt ten times more so now.

The crowd was beginning to scatter, leaving that stranger alone on the boat. Leaning over the railing of the boat, he called after them, saying—

"Friends, if there are any of you who love the Lord Jesus Christ, I am your brother."

In a moment half a dozen of them were at his side. They shook him warmly by the hand, and bade him welcome to their homes.

How different Cincinnati seemed to that stranger

THE KING IN HIS BEAUTY.

now, from what it did a moment before! The *place* indeed was the same; but oh, how different the *company* seemed! He was among friends now, and that made him feel at home.

And so it will be with us when we get to heaven. Jesus will know and love every one who enters there. He will introduce us to those who are there, and they will all love us, because we love Jesus. Angels, and Christians, old and young, men, women, and children, will all make one great happy family.

"Thine eyes shall see the King in His beauty." There will be beauty in the *place*, and beauty in the *company*.

*But there is a third thing that will have more to do with the beauty of heaven, than either the place, or the company—and that is—*THE PERSON AND PRESENCE OF JESUS.

But what shall I say about this point of our subject? It is easy enough to talk about the *place*, where heaven is to be. It is easy enough, too, to talk about the *company* that will be there; but when we come to think about the *person*, and *presence of Jesus*, in heaven, who is able to speak on such a subject?

There was a celebrated painter once, who was making a picture of Jesus, in the midst of His twelve apostles. In arranging the picture he concluded to paint the apostles first, and not begin with their Master till he had finished them. As he went on with the picture, he tried to do the very best he could with each of the apostles. He took the greatest pains with their figures, their positions, their dress and their faces. As he went on with his work he was very well pleased with it. After finishing the apostles he began with the person of Jesus. He got on very well with this, till he came to the head and face of our blessed Lord. Then he laid down his brush and paused. He felt that the face of Jesus ought to be made to appear as much more beautiful than His disciples, as the sun is more glorious than the stars. But how could he do this? He had tried so hard to make the disciples look well, that he felt he had no power left to make their Master appear as much superior to them as He ought to appear. And so he finished the person of Jesus all but the head, and then painted Him with a white mantle thrown over His head. He thought that when persons came to look at his painting, they could *imagine* what the face of Jesus ought to be, better than he could represent it by painting.

And I feel very much as that painter did, when I come to speak about—*the person and presence of Jesus in heaven.* All who love Jesus here on earth, agree in saying that from what they know of Him now, He is—" the chief among ten thousand, and *altogether lovely.*" Then how will He appear when our eyes come to "see the King in His beauty," in heaven? Just look for a moment at what some good Christian men have said about Jesus, from what they knew of Him, here in this world.

When John Newton was thinking of Him, he said—

" How sweet the name of Jesus sounds
In a believer's ears!

> It soothes his sorrows, heals his wounds,
> And drives away his fears."

A good Roman Catholic, who lived more than six hundred years ago, expressed his feelings thus—

> "Jesus, the very thought of Thee,
> With sweetness fills my breast,
> *But sweeter far Thy face to see,*
> And in Thy bosom rest.
>
> "Nor voice can sing, nor heart can frame,
> Nor can the memory find
> A sweeter sound than Thy blest name,
> O Saviour of mankind."

When Dr. Doddridge was thinking about Him he said—

> "Jesus, I love Thy charming name,
> 'Tis music to my ear;
> Fain would I sound it out so loud
> That earth and heaven might hear.
>
> "All my capacious powers can wish
> In Thee doth richly meet,
> Not to my eyes is light so dear,
> Nor friendship half so sweet."

And Charles Wesley when thinking about Him burst out thus—

> "Oh, for a thousand tongues to sing
> My great Redeemer's praise!
> The glories of my God and King,
> The triumphs of His grace!
>
> "Jesus! the name that calms our fears,
> That bids our sorrows cease;
> 'Tis music in the sinner's ears,
> 'Tis life, and health, and peace."

When such men get to heaven it will not be the

riches that adorn the *place*, nor the perfection of the *company* there, that will make up its chief beauty to them. No, but it will be the *person and presence of Jesus* there that will constitute the charm, the glory, the fulness of heaven's joy to their souls. And this is just what Dr. Muhlenberg speaks of in that beautiful hymn of his, in which heaven is spoken of as a place—

> "Where the saints of all ages in harmony meet,
> Their Saviour and brethren transported to greet,
> While the anthems of rapture unceasingly roll,
> And *the smile of the Lord is the feast of the soul.*"

The person and presence of Jesus, and "the smile of the Lord," both mean the same thing.

We have one *description* given us in the Bible, of the person and presence of Jesus in heaven. The Apostle John saw a vision of heaven. He saw "the King in His beauty," and this is what he says about it:—

"I saw seven golden candlesticks: And in the midst of the seven candlesticks, one like unto the Son of Man, clothed with a garment down to the foot, and girded with a golden girdle. His head and His hair were white like wool, as white as snow; and His eyes were as a flame of fire; And His feet like unto fine brass, as if they burned in a furnace; and His voice as the sound of many waters. And He had in His right hand seven stars; and out of His mouth went a sharp two-edged sword; and His countenance was as the sun shining in his strength" (Rev. i. 12-17).

And then, in addition to this *description*, in another place in the Bible, we have an *illustration* of how the person and presence of Jesus will appear in heaven. I refer here to the Transfiguration of our Saviour. There is Jesus on the top of Mount Tabor, if that was the place. His three disciples, Peter, and James, and John, are with Him. As they look at Him, they see a wondrous change take place in His appearance. He is transfigured before them, His raiment becomes exceeding white as snow, a whiteness such as no one in the world could impart. His countenance changes too, till it shines like the sun—and a glory is beaming around Him such as was never seen in the sun. And Moses and Elias are seen there in glory too—and the voice of God is heard speaking there. This transfiguration scene took place in order to give us an idea of what heaven will be. When our "eyes see the King in His beauty," we shall see Him as He appeared on the Mount of Transfiguration.

And then, all the beauty that we see, in this world around us, is but a glimpse, or reflection, of the richer beauty that we shall see in Jesus. The beauty of the sun, and stars, and light; the beauty of the sky, the clouds, the seasons; the beauty of mountains, hills, and plains; the beauty of birds, and beasts, and insects; the beauty of trees, and plants, and flowers,—and all the beauty that we see everywhere, is only a shadow, a type, or reflection, of the beauty that we shall see in Jesus when we get to heaven. We shall find the *place* glorious, and the *company* perfect; but the chief beauty and blessedness of heaven will be in the *person and presence of Jesus.*

A Sunday-school teacher was visiting one of her scholars who was soon to die. The sick child was a Christian. She expressed an earnest desire to go to heaven.

"Why do you wish so much to go there, Mary?" asked her teacher.

"Because Jesus is there, and I long so to see Him."

"But suppose, Mary, that when you get there, you should find that Jesus was going out of heaven, what would you do?"

"I would go out with Him"—was her quick reply. She felt that there could be no heaven to her without Jesus.

"Thine eyes shall see the King in His beauty." Remember, there are three things with which this beauty will be connected. These are—the *place*—the *company*—and the *person and presence of Jesus*.

There is one very important lesson we should learn from this subject; it is this: *we must learn to love Jesus here, or else His presence in heaven will not make us happy.*

We see this lesson illustrated in the Hindoo fable about the crane. The fable says that one day a crane was contentedly eating snails in a marsh. As she was thus engaged a bird flew down from the sky, and lighted near her. "Where do you come from?" asked the crane. "From heaven," was the answer.

"What have you seen in heaven?" asked the crane. "Everything that can make people happy." And then the bird went on and described some of the joys of that blessed place.

"Have they any snails in heaven?" asked the crane,

as much as to say—"I don't care to be in any place where there are no snails."

"You vulgar, low-bred creature!" said the bird, and flew away offended.

Now suppose that this crane had been taken to heaven; would it have been happy there? Not at all. It would have been longing, all the time, for the marsh where it used to wade and catch snails. We must be *prepared* for heaven, if we hope to be happy there. And there is only one true preparation. This is—*learning to know and love Jesus*. If we really love Him, we shall be perfectly happy to be where He is. And when our "eyes see the King in His beauty," that will satisfy us for ever. We shall want nothing else. *That* will be a perfect heaven to us.

II.

THE BEAUTY OF THE KING.

"THE KINGDOM OF GOD IS—RIGHTEOUSNESS, AND PEACE, AND JOY IN THE HOLY GHOST."—*Romans* xiv. 17.

II.

THE BEAUTY OF THE KING.

Our last sermon was from a text that took us up to heaven, and led us to look at "the King in His beauty." Now we have a text that brings us down to earth again, and leads us to look at the beauty in the King. Jesus will have a kingdom in our world that will be wondrously beautiful. It will be different from any kingdom ever yet known in the world. This is what Jesus taught us to pray for, when He put into that wonderful prayer—"The Lord's Prayer"—these words, "Thy kingdom come." But I am not going to talk of *that* kingdom now. The Bible says a great many things concerning it. Some of these are hard to be understood, and good and wise men have very different opinions about the meaning of those things.

But Jesus is a king *now*, in one sense. He rules in the hearts of His people. He has a kingdom there. And there is very much that is interesting and beautiful about this kingdom. This is what the Apostle Paul is speaking of, in our text, when he says—"The kingdom of God is—not meat and drink, but righteousness, and peace, and joy in the Holy Ghost."

Jesus is often spoken of in the Bible as a King. David, in the Book of Psalms, represents God as saying of Him—"Yet have I set *my King* upon my holy hill of Zion" (Ps. ii. 6). The prophet Isaiah often speaks of Jesus as a King. This is what he means when he says—"Behold a King shall reign, and prosper; and—shall be as a refuge from the storm, a covert from the tempest; as rivers of water in a dry place, as the shadow of a great rock in a weary land" (Isa. xxxii. 1, 2). And when the angel Gabriel came to the virgin mother of Jesus, to tell her about His birth, he spoke of Him as a King. "And the Lord God," these were the angel's words, "shall give unto Him the throne of His father David, and He shall reign over the house of Jacob for ever" (Luke i. 32).

Now let us look at Jesus from this point of view and see what beauty there is in Him as a King. *The beauty of Jesus as a King!* this is our subject. And the question we must try to answer is this; what sort of a kingdom does Jesus have now? or, what does He do for those who belong to His kingdom? And when we understand what this is—we shall see what great beauty there is in Jesus as a King.

In our present text, the Apostle Paul tells us of three things that Jesus, as a King, does for His people now.

The first thing that Jesus does for those who belong to His kingdom is—to MAKE THEM GOOD.

The Apostle Paul tells us in our text that the kingdom of Jesus is a kingdom of righteousness. Righteousness here means goodness. And what we are taught is that Jesus is a King who makes all His subjects, or those that belong to His kingdom, good. Oh, if all *earthly* kings were able to do this, and were really trying to do it, how much beauty we should see in them! But they cannot do this. Really good kings like King Solomon in Israel, or Alfred the Great, or Edward the Sixth in England, try to do good to their people in some way or other. But as for undertaking to make the people belonging to their kingdoms all good, this is what they never pretend to do. It would be impossible. But what is impossible with earthly kings, Jesus, the heavenly King, really does. He is the good King. His kingdom is a good kingdom, and every one who belongs to it He makes good. The prophet Isaiah is speaking of this kingdom when he says—"Thy people shall be *all righteous,*" or good (Isa. lx. 21). And Jesus tells us how He will do this. He says, "A new heart also will I give them, and a new spirit will I put within them" (Ezek. xxxvi. 26). "And I will put my law in their inward parts, and write it in their hearts, and I will be their God, and they shall be my people" (Jer. xxxi. 33). And when Jesus does this for all His people it may well be said that He makes them good. Now let us look at some examples, or specimens, of people who are the subjects of this King, and of the way in which He makes them good.

THE PENITENT BOY THIEF.

On a heap of chips and shavings, in a garret, a Christian man, visiting among the poor of London, found a boy about ten years old. He was pale, but with a very sweet face.

"What are you doing here, my boy?" he asked.

"Hush! hush! I'm hiding."

"Hiding? What for?" The poor boy rolled up his ragged shirt-sleeve, and showed his thin white arm all black and blue with bruises.

"Who was it beat you like that?"

"Don't tell—but my father did it."

"What for?"

"Father gets drunk, and beats me because I won't steal."

"Did you ever steal?"

"Yes, sir; I used to steal once."

"Then why don't you steal now?"

"Because I went to the Sunday-school, and there I learned about the God of heaven, and how His law says, *Thou shalt not steal.* I will never steal any more, even if father kills me."

That little boy thief had become one of the subjects of Jesus, and He had made him good.

HOW MATTIE LEARNED TO SERVE GOD.

A little girl, named Mattie, made up her mind to try and become a Christian. She got up the next morning, and resolved to look out for some great thing to do, in order to show her love to Jesus. But the day passed away without her finding anything great to do; and at the close of the day she felt very much discouraged. So she put on her bonnet, and went to her Aunt Jennie's, at the other end of the village. She sat down on the piazza, and leaned her head on her hand, and seemed very thoughtful. By and by, her aunt came and sat down by her side. She took hold of her hand and gently said—

"What's the matter with you, Mattie?"

"Why, auntie," she said, "I want to serve the Lord Jesus, and I have been looking all the day to find some great thing to do for Him, but I have not found any."

"Ah! Mattie dear," said her aunt, "you are just making the same mistake that so many other persons have made before."

"What mistake, auntie?"

"Why the mistake of thinking you can only serve God by doing *great* things. Now suppose, that instead of waiting all day for something great to do, you had begun in the morning by asking Jesus to help you to be useful; and then had tried to help mother in sweeping the room; or amusing the baby; or helping Mary in the kitchen; and then had gone to work and learned that long lesson well, you would have found plenty to do all day."

"Well, auntie, but those are such little things."

"I know it, Mattie; but then life is made up of little

things. Now I want you to go home, and try this plan to-morrow, and see how it works."

Mattie went home wiser than she came. She began the next day as her auntie told her.

Before leaving her room, in the morning, she found work to do for Jesus. When her mother came up to make Mattie's bed, she was surprised to find the bed made, and the room all in the nicest order. When Mattie went downstairs she found work to do for Jesus there. All day long, wherever she went, there was something for her to do. And the thought that she was doing it for Jesus made it all sweet, and pleasant to her. She was as busy as a bee, and as bright as a sunbeam all the day.

At the close of the afternoon, when she was going up to her room, her mother laid her hand gently on her shoulder and said, "Mattie, darling, you have been a real comfort and blessing to me to-day."

This filled Mattie's eyes with tears, but they were tears of joy and gladness. And as she knelt down in her room to thank God for helping her to serve Him, the sun never shone upon a happier girl than Mattie was that evening.

And here we see how Jesus makes His people good.

And sometimes, when people have gone very far astray, Jesus makes them good by His grace, when nothing else could do it.

HOW OLD JIM DRAYTON WAS MADE GOOD.

There was a little town, in New England, in which a miserable drunkard lived. Everybody there knew him as "Old Jim Drayton." He had once been a respectable mechanic. Then he had a neat little cottage as his home, and his family were very happy. But, since he had taken to drink, everything had gone to ruin. The furniture had been sold for liquor. The broken window-panes were patched with pieces of newspaper, or stuffed with bundles of rags and bunches of straw. His wife looked sorrowful and broken-hearted, and his children were covered with rags.

Jim himself went reeling about the village with a battered hat, and ragged clothes, and a bloated, stupid-looking face. He went to the tavern, one New Year's eve, intending to drink out the old year. The bar-keeper was busy when he went in, and he sat down in a corner by himself.

Presently two young men came in. They called for some beer. While they were drinking it one of them said, "I say, Bill, did you hear that Old Jim Drayton had cut his throat?"

"It's good news, if it's true," said the other. "No one will miss the old sot, not even his family. They'd be better off without him. He's just the lowest drunkard in town."

"Yes, I've often wondered why he didn't jump into the river," said the other. "If I ever get as low, and ragged, and mean as Jim Drayton, I'll shoot myself."

Old Jim heard every word. He was quite sober. He leaned his back against the wall, pulled his hat over his face, and thought of what he heard. "Have I got so low as this?" he said to himself. "Would my death be a relief to my family, and to the town? Then it's time for me to stop." As he sat there he offered this silent prayer—"God help me to quit drinking, and be a new man!"

Just then the barkeeper sung out—"O Jim! do you want a drink?"

Jim sprang to his feet, and said, "No, I'm going to swear off from drinking from this hour!"

"That's good," they all exclaimed; "Old Jim Drayton going to quit drinking—ha! ha! ha!"

"I'll do it, by the help of God," said Jim, striking his fist on the counter. Then he left the tavern.

He went directly home. At the gate, which led to his dwelling, he stopped for a moment, and saw what a wretched-looking home it was; and how different from what it had once been! As his wife heard the door open, she turned away to hide herself, afraid to meet him in his drunken wrath.

"Mary, come here," he said as he closed the door, and held out his hand—"I am not drunk to-night."

She came slowly up to him, wondering what it meant.

"Mary," he said, as he clasped her hand, "I haven't drunk a drop to-night."

"O James!" she exclaimed, as she threw her arms round his neck, and sobbed aloud.

"'God help me to quit drinking, and be a new man!'"

"They call me Old Jim Drayton, and say I'm only a burden to my family, and the town, and that I can't reform," he went on, "but I'm going to stop drinking—I have stopped." His poor wife's heart was too full to speak. "From this night, as long as I live," he continued, "I'll be James Drayton again,—sober—steady—a kind husband, a good father. Now, Mary, go wake up the children, and let us all pray together."

"Is father going to kill us?" they whispered as their mother woke them up.

"No—no—he's sober now, he's going to be a dear good father again," she sobbed.

At midnight the voice of prayer, broken by loud sobs, was heard in that drunkard's home, and Old Jim Drayton, kneeling in the midst of his weeping family, said—"God forgive me for the past; and help me to be a good husband and father for the future."

And God did hear him, and help him too. And from that hour he kept his vow; and became a sober, industrious, useful man. And the grace of God, which was sufficient to reform, and save, a wretched drunkard like Jim Drayton, and make a good man of him, is able to do the same for any one.

There is great beauty in Jesus as a King, because of what He does for all who belong to His kingdom. The first thing He does for them is *to make them good*.

The second thing He does for them is to make them— PEACEFUL.

"The kingdom of God is righteousness and—*peace*."

Jesus, the head of this kingdom, is the Prince of

Peace. The Gospel which tells about this kingdom is —"*The Gospel of Peace.*" The ministers of this kingdom are sent out—"*preaching peace* through Jesus Christ." And the people who belong to this kingdom are commanded to—"*follow peace with all men.*"

This kingdom of peace is intended, by and by, to fill the whole world. Then, we are told that men will "beat their swords into ploughshares, and their spears into pruning-hooks, and the nations shall learn war no more." Then earthquakes will no more alarm and destroy. Storms will no more burst; nor tempests blow; and all nature will be at peace. Even the wild animals will lose their fierceness, and share in this blessing of peace. Isaiah says, at that time—"The wolf also shall dwell with the lamb, and the leopard shall lie down with the kid; and the calf and the young lion and the fatling together; and a little child shall lead them" (Isa. **xi.** 6).

And *now*, before that "good time" comes, Jesus teaches all who wish to serve Him, and belong to His kingdom, to be kind, loving, and gentle; and try to make peace with those about them. Now let us look at some examples of the way in which those who have Jesus for their King try to make peace.

FREDDIE'S PRAYER.

A little boy, named Freddie, was going home at the close of a day in winter. A mantle of pure white snow was spread over the fields and woods as he walked

THE BEAUTY OF THE KING. 37

along. It was about sunset, and as the beams of the sun fell on the landscape they covered it with golden glory. Everything around seemed beautiful. There was no cloud in the sky, but there was a cloud on Freddie's face. When he got into the house he stamped his foot, and seemed to be very angry about something or other.

"What's the matter, Freddie?" asked his mother.

"It's that ugly old boy, Bennie Jones, mother. I hate him. He's always hurting me—and just on purpose too."

"But," said his mother, "nobody teaches him better. Freddie must pray for him."

"But Freddie won't,"—and his eyes flashed fire. His mother said nothing more about it then, but talked about something else.

Pretty soon came bedtime, and the bedtime story; for Freddie's mother always had some nice Bible story to tell him before he went to sleep. This night it was the story of Jesus on Calvary. She spoke of the wicked cruelty of the men who mocked Him, and scourged Him, and nailed Him to the cross. She told of His dreadful sufferings, as He hung bleeding there; yet of His patience under all, and of His wonderful love for His murderers, which led Him to pray for them, in the midst of His pain and sorrow, and say—

"Father, forgive them, for they know not what they do."

Freddie listened eagerly till his mother had finished. Then he gently said, "I'll say my prayers now, mother, please; and I think *I'll pray for Bennie Jones first.*"

So the little prayer was offered, and Freddie went to bed, with a face bright as sunshine. Every unkind feeling was taken out of his heart. The spirit of Jesus, which is a spirit of peace, was filling it. There is beauty in Jesus as a King, because He makes His people loving and peaceful.

BEATING SATAN.

The Apostle Paul says—" If it be possible, as much as lieth in *you*, live peaceably with all men." It always takes two people to make a quarrel. It is not the first angry word, or the first blow, that leads to a quarrel. It is the second word, or the second blow, that always makes the quarrel. If we refuse to speak the second word, or strike the second blow, then the persons who want to make the quarrel will have it *all to themselves.* And as the boys say—" There's no fun in this;" and so this is the way to prevent quarrels.

Some time ago, a man was converted in New Hampshire, and afterwards became a minister of the Gospel. Before becoming a Christian he was well known, in the neighbourhood where he lived, as a man of very violent temper, over which he had no control. At the very time of his conversion he had an unsettled dispute with one of his neighbours. They had often talked it over, and it always ended in their both getting very angry about it. When this man's neighbour heard that he had joined the Church, he called at his house to talk over their old dispute, and to see if he could not make him angry, and get up a quarrel with him, as easily as he used to do before he became a Christian. He began at once by abusing him with great violence, and throwing all the blame of the old quarrel upon him.

Not an angry word was spoken in reply. This provoked him more than ever. He cursed and swore in a dreadful manner. Still the Christian was calm and silent. Then enraged beyond measure at the man's coolness, his angry neighbour raised his cane, and struck him a blow with it. And still the Christian did not his temper, but remained calm and quiet.

"Why," exclaimed the angry man in his astonishment, "you beat old Satan himself!"

"That's what I mean to do," said the good man coolly, "and this is just the way in which I'm going to do it."

There was no second angry word, or blow here, and so there was no quarrel. The angry man went back to his home. But as he went he said to himself—

"Well, there must be something in religion more than I know about. I guess it's time for me to look into it."

Oh, there is beauty in the King who can make His people practise "the things that make for peace" in such a way as this!

THE NEIGHBOURS AND THE HENS.

A Christian man in New Jersey belonged to this kingdom of peace, and he gives us this account of his own experience about the effect produced by a patient, peaceful example.

"I once had a number of fowls. Generally they were kept shut up. But, one spring, I concluded to clip their wings so that they could not fly, and let them run in my yard. One day, when I came home to dinner, I found that one of my neighbours had been there, full of anger, to say that my hens had been in his garden, and that he had killed several of them, and had thrown them into my yard. It made me very angry to think that he should have killed my beautiful hens, that I valued so much. I determined at once to be revenged. I would go to law with him, or make him smart for it in some way.

"I sat down and ate my dinner as calmly as I could. Before dinner was over I became cooler. I said to myself—'Is it the best way for a Christian man to quarrel with his neighbour, and make a lasting enemy of him about such a trifling thing as two or three hens? Jesus said—"Learn of me." How would Jesus have me act? What would He do if He were in my place?'

"So I changed my mind about the matter. After dinner I called at my neighbour's house. He was in his garden. I went out and found him chasing one of my hens, with a stick in his hand, trying to kill it. I said to him, 'Neighbour, look here.'

"He turned round and looked at me. With his face all flaming with anger, he exclaimed—'You have injured me, sir. I'll kill every hen you've got, if I can catch them. They have ruined my garden, sir.'

"'I am very sorry for it,' said I. 'I do not wish to injure you; I see now that I have made a great mistake in letting my hens out. I ask your pardon, and am willing to pay you six times the damage they have done.'

"You ought to have seen that man. He was completely confounded. As the sailors say, 'he was taken all aback.' He did not know what to make of it. He looked up to the sky, then down to the ground; then he looked at me, then at his stick, then at the poor hen he was trying to kill, and he had not a word to say.

"'Tell me now,' I said, 'what is the damage, and I will pay you sixfold, and my hens shall never trouble you any more. I leave it entirely with you to say what I shall pay. I cannot afford to lose the good-will of my neighbours, and quarrel with them for hens or anything else.'

"By this time the man had found his tongue. 'Neighbour,' said he, 'I'm a great fool. The damage isn't worth talking about. Won't you pardon me? I thank you for the lesson you have taught me about good sense and practical wisdom.'"

Here we see what the spirit of the Gospel is. How much beauty there is in the King who can make His people act in such a way as this! The second thing that Jesus does for His people is to make them peaceful.

This shows us the beauty there is in Jesus as a King.

But there is a third thing that Jesus does for His people. He makes them—HAPPY.

And here, too, we see what beauty there is in Him as a King.

What a wonderful thing it would be, if any earthly king had the power of making all the people belonging to his kingdom happy! This is what no king ever undertook to do. But Jesus is able and willing to do it. And this is what is meant in our text, when it says that—"the kingdom of God is"—or consists of—"joy in the Holy Ghost." Joy in the Holy Ghost means the best kind of happiness. Jesus prayed for His people—John xvii. 13—that they might all be filled with the same sort of joy that He has. *That* must certainly be the best kind of happiness.

Let us see what Jesus does to make His people happy.

LITTLE TANGLES.

There was once a king, who employed a great many of his people to work for him as weavers. The silk, and the patterns, were all given by the king. He told the workers, when they met with any trouble, to send for him, and he would come and help them; and that they never need be afraid of troubling him.

Many persons—men, women, and children,—were busy at the looms. Among these was a little girl, who always seemed bright, and cheerful, over her work, though she was often left to do it all alone. One day some

THE BEAUTY OF THE KING.

of the weavers were very much troubled about their work. Their threads were tangled and broken, and the work they were finishing was not like the patterns given them to copy. Then they gathered round the cheerful little girl, and said—

"Tell us how it is that you are always so happy in your work, while we are constantly getting into trouble?"

"Why, I always send to the king when I am in trouble," said the little weaver. "You know he told us we might do so."

"So we do," they said, "every night and morning."

"Ah!" said the child, "but I send directly, as soon as I find that I get into a little tangle. So I always get help at once, and this saves a great deal of trouble."

This was the secret of her being so cheerful and happy. And this is what Jesus wants us to do. He says in one place—"Call upon me, in the day of trouble, and I will deliver thee; and thou shalt glorify me" (Ps. l. 15). And in another place He says—"Casting *all your care on Him, for He careth for you*" (1 Peter v. 7).

It is a beautiful thing to think of Jesus as a King who is able and willing to help His people when they are in trouble. This is one of the ways in which He makes them happy.

THE ROBBER CRIPPLE.

Some years ago an English missionary was stationed in Asia Minor. On one occasion, he sent two men connected with his mission on a journey, through the Taurus Mountains. They took with them a lot of Bibles, which they were to give away in the villages, wherever they could find people who were willing to receive them.

One day these men stopped under a tree to rest. While they were resting, one of these men took out a Bible, and read a chapter for himself and his companion. It was the third chapter of St. John, about the conversation between Jesus and Nicodemus.

Sitting by the hedge, near them, was an old man. He was a beggar and a cripple. His hands were withered, and his elbows stiff, and only a few rags covered his body. But more than this, he was a very wicked man. He had been a robber and a murderer. He had been connected with many scenes of violence and blood. But now he was old, and poor, and friendless. He was as wretched a man as could be found anywhere, with no hope either for this world or the next.

Well, this wretched old man was sitting near the Bible distributers on that day. He heard the chapter from the Bible read. He had never heard the Bible before. It had a wonderful effect upon him. The 16th verse of that chapter, especially, took great hold of his mind: "*God so loved the world that He gave His only begotten Son, that whosoever believeth on Him should not perish, but have everlasting life.*" He thought these were the sweetest words he had ever heard. He repeated them to himself, so as to fix them in his memory. The Bible men went on their way, without taking any notice of the old beggar cripple. But he was saying those wonderful words, over and over, to himself. The thought that God loved him, and cared for him, softened his hard heart. He thought about his sins, and was filled with distress. He cried for mercy all the time. He spoke to the people in the village about the wonderful words he had heard. But they only laughed at him, and thought he was crazy.

Still he kept crying to God, confessing his sins, and praying for mercy. And God heard and answered his prayer. He found peace and pardon. This filled him with joy. The poor old lame beggar, was as happy as the day was long. He was as poor as ever; and as lame as ever; but the thought that Jesus loved him, and had died to save him, made him happy.

After awhile the missionary came along where the Bible distributers had been. He had heard of the old beggar, and thought he would try and comfort him. But instead of this the old man comforted the missionary, and taught him a new lesson, about the wonders of God's grace and love. Here was an old man, who had never seen a missionary before; had never heard a sermon; and never attended a religious meeting, but who was made perfectly happy in the midst of all his poverty, loneliness, and infirmity, by simply reading God's Word, and having faith in Jesus as his Saviour.

Oh, there is wonderful beauty in Jesus as a King, when we see how **He can make** people happy under such circumstances.

HAPPY IN DEATH.

There is no time when we are in greater need of something to make us happy than when we are going to die. Yet Jesus can take away the sting from death, and make His people so happy that they do not fear death.

Some time ago there was a young man in England, about eighteen years of age, who met his death suddenly and unexpectedly; but who was peaceful and happy in meeting it, by the help that Jesus gave him. This young man was the son of a clergyman. His father's house was near the sea. He was very fond of rambling on the sea-shore, and searching for beautiful specimens of seaweed. One day he was on the shore, as usual, gathering specimens. The tide was low. There was a ledge of rocks very full of seaweeds. These rocks could only be reached at the lowest stage of the tide. The young man got on these rocks. Here he found great quantities of the most beautiful specimens. He was so much interested in gathering them that he quite forgot to watch how the tide was coming in. When he had gathered as much as he wanted of the seaweed, he looked round to see about getting off from the rocks; and, then, to his surprise, he found the water had risen so high between him and the shore, that it was impossible for him to get off. He could not swim, and it was too deep for him to wade. He looked about him; but there was no one in sight. At the top of his voice he shouted—"Help! help!" but there was none near

THE BEAUTY OF THE KING.

enough to hear. Then he saw that he must die. Taking out his pocket Bible he wrote on the blank leaf as follows:—" In danger—surrounded by water: if help does not come soon, I must be drowned. But Jesus, to whom I gave myself five years ago, is with me. I am perfectly happy. May He bless and comfort my beloved parents, and bring my dear little brothers and sisters to Himself, so that we may all meet in heaven."

Then he calmly waited till the rising waters swept him from the rocks, and he was taken to heaven. The next day his body was found, and the hearts of his sorrowing parents were greatly comforted by those last sweet words written in his Bible.

It is a beautiful thing to think of Jesus as a King who can make His people happy under circumstances so sad as those in which this young man found himself. No one else can do this but Jesus. He is a King who can make His people *good*, and *peaceful*, and *happy*. And for these reasons we may well speak of the wonderful beauty there is in Jesus as a King. And if we learn to love and serve Him, we shall find that He is not only beautiful in Himself, but that He has the power to make us beautiful too, for we shall " see Him as He is, and *shall be like Him.*"

III.

THE KING IN THE BEAUTY OF HIS KINGDOM.

"HIS KINGDOM RULETH OVER ALL."—*Psalm* ciii. 19.

III.

THE KING IN THE BEAUTY OF HIS KINGDOM.

We have spoken of the beauty of Jesus as a King. He makes all His people good, and peaceable, and happy. And a king who really can do this for all his subjects, appears very beautiful to us. And the words of David in our present text call us to look at the *kingdom* of Jesus. He *has* a kingdom *now*. The Bible tells us that He is seated at the right hand of God the Father. And He sits there as King. "The government is upon His shoulder." It is easier for us to think of Jesus as a poor man, than as a great King. We read of Him as "the man of sorrows, and acquainted with grief;" we know that He was so poor that, "though the foxes had holes, and the birds of the air had nests, yet He had not where to lay His head." We think of Him as healing the sick, and raising the dead, and working many miracles as "He went about doing good." All this is easy for us to think about; but it is not so easy for us to think about Jesus as having a great kingdom; yet this is what we must now try to do.

When we hear people talking about governments, or

kingdoms, we are very apt to think, " Well, these are not things that are of any importance to us as children. Men and women may attend to these things; but they are not for *us* to think of, or care much about." Well, if it were the kingdom of England, or the government of France, or Germany, or Russia, or China, that we were talking about, then it would be true. We, as children, would have no interest in those kingdoms or governments. It would make very little difference to us whether those kingdoms were good or bad. But when we come to talk about the kingdom that Jesus has, it is very different. We are all interested in this kingdom. It has something to do with every one of us. From the oldest scholar in one of our Bible-classes, down to the youngest scholar in the infant school, we should all wish to know about this kingdom. This kingdom has a great deal to do with every one of us. We should all try to find out what sort of a kingdom it is. And this is what we wish now to speak of. I want to show that there is great beauty in the kingdom of Jesus. This is our subject now: *The beauty of Christ's kingdom.*

There are *three* reasons why it is beautiful.

*In the first place, the kingdom of Jesus is a beautiful kingdom because it rules over—*ALL THE GREATEST THINGS.

One of the greatest things that we know of, is this world that we live on. If we could take a line, and go all round the outside of the world, and measure it, we should find that line about twenty-four thousand miles long. If we could bore a hole, right through the earth, from just where we stand to the other side of it, and then drop a line through, we should find that line—measuring the diameter of the earth—would be about eight thousand miles in length. This vast world is full of rocks, and sand, and earth, and water. How big this world is! How hard it must be to move it! Why, if the world should stand still, all the men that ever lived, with all the horses to help them, and all the steam engines ever made, if they were all put together, could not move the world a single inch; no, nor the hundredth part of an inch. But Jesus, in His beautiful kingdom, moves this great world a great deal easier than you, or I, can bend our little finger.

But though this world, that we live in, seems so great to us, it is really a very little world, compared to some others. Yonder is the great sun, that shines upon us every day. That is a world too. And it is a much larger world than ours. It is so much larger that a million of worlds like ours could be put inside of it. For us to say a million is a very easy thing. But it is not so easy to understand just what a million means. Suppose we should begin, to-morrow morning at six o'clock, to count. And suppose that we should count about as fast as the clock ticks—one, two, three, four, and so on. And then suppose we should go on counting, at that rate, till six o'clock at night, without stopping to eat, or to drink, or to rest. This would be counting for a day of twelve hours. We could only count, in this way, about forty-three thousand a day. And at this rate it would take us twenty-three days, or more than three weeks, to count a million, spending twelve hours each day in the work. Now suppose there was a great hole in the side of the sun, like a bung-hole in a hogshead. And suppose that God should set you and me to fill up the sun, by dropping into it worlds like ours, just as we might fill up a hogshead by dropping pebbles into the bung-hole. And suppose that we were able to pick up worlds like ours as easily as we can pick up pebbles. Well now, we take our stand by that hole in the side of the sun, and try to fill it up. We begin to drop in worlds. As fast as the clock ticks, we drop them in—one, two, three, four, five, six. Sixty a minute—thirty-six hundred an hour, forty-three thousand for a day of twelve hours, we keep on at this work. It would take us more than twenty-three days, working on at the same rate, to fill up the sun by putting into it a million of worlds like ours. Oh, how wonderfully great that sun must be! And yet Jesus, in His kingdom, rules that sun. He tells it to shine; and it does shine. He tells it to keep on shining; and it keeps on shining. When we look up at the sky at night, you know how many stars we see shining there. Many of them are worlds as large as our sun. Some of them are larger. But the kingdom of Jesus rules over all those worlds. They all obey Him. They move just where He tells them to move. They do just what He tells them to do.

And then let us look away from the worlds to the *angels*. They are wonderful for their greatness. David says—"They *excel* in strength" (Psalm ciii. 20). Samson, we know, was the strongest man that ever lived. But if the world were full of men like Samson, one angel would have more strength than all of them put together. Just think, for a moment, of some of the things which we know that angels have done; and which show us how wonderful their strength is.

When God wished to destroy Sodom and Gomorrah, He sent an angel to do it. It was an angel that let loose that storm of fire, by which the guilty cities of the plain were burnt up and destroyed.

When God wished to deliver the children of Israel out of Egypt, He sent an angel to do it. The angel passed over the land of Egypt that night; and with his unseen sword smote all the first-born of the Egyptians both of man and beast. Some one was dead in every family; and one long, loud wail of sorrow was heard all through the land.

It was an angel that blew the trumpet when God came down to give the Israelites the law on the top of Mount Sinai. And the blast of that trumpet made the earth shake, and the mountains tremble all around.

When God wished to deliver Jerusalem from the army of the Assyrians that was encamped against it, He sent an angel to do it. That angel passed over the Assyrian army at night, while they were asleep. He made no noise in passing; but quietly and silently he breathed, as it were, upon them. And with that breath he slew a hundred and eighty-five thousand men.

When God wished to deliver the apostle Peter out of prison, He sent an angel to do it. This angel came into the prison where Peter was sleeping, and awoke him. Then he touched his chains, and they fell off from his limbs. As they were coming out of the prison, they came to a great iron gate leading into the city. This was made fast by bolts and bars. Before the angel touched it, before he came near to it, he made this gate open, in spite of all its fastenings, as if it were of its own accord.

Here we see what single angels have done. But, when Jesus was going to be crucified, He said that if He should ask the Father in heaven, He would send Him more than twelve legions of angels to help Him, and deliver Him from His enemies. That would have been more than seventy thousand angels. All the angels in heaven worship Jesus. They all serve and obey Him. His kingdom ruleth over all the angels of heaven.

And then, *everything else that is great and powerful is ruled by Him*. Storms and tempests, winds and waves, heat and cold, frost and snow, are His servants. His kingdom ruleth over all these. They all obey Him. They do just what He tells them to do.

When Jesus was on the Sea of Galilee in a storm He fell asleep while the storm was raging. His disciples thought the vessel was going to sink. In their fright they awoke Him, and begged Him to save them from being drowned. Jesus got up, went to the side of the vessel, and quietly spoke to the howling winds and foaming waves, saying — "Peace ; be still." They heard Him. They obeyed Him ; "*and immediately there was a great calm.*" And Jesus has just the same power to control winds, and waves, and all things now that He had then. His kingdom ruleth over all the greatest things. He has "all power in heaven and on earth." As the prophet Jeremiah says (ch. xxxii. 17)—"He made the heaven and the earth by His great power, and His outstretched arm; and nothing is too hard for Him."

A vessel was at sea in a terrible storm some time ago. The captain gave up all hope of being able to save the ship, and told the passengers to prepare for the worst. Some were crying aloud and wringing their hands; others were calling upon God to save them. Among these was a Christian man who remained perfectly calm.

"How can you be so quiet in the midst of this fearful storm?" asked one of his fellow-passengers.

"My Father in heaven is ruling this storm," said the Christian. "He can keep the vessel from sinking if He sees best. If I sink, I shall still be in my Father's hand. I know I am safe there. Why should I be afraid?"

That was the right use to make of the subject we are now talking about. The kingdom of Jesus is a beautiful kingdom, because it rules over all the greatest things.

But the kingdom of Jesus is a beautiful kingdom, in the second place, because it rules over—ALL THE SMALLEST THINGS.

On the one hand, nothing is so great that He is unable to manage it; and on the other hand, nothing is so little that He ever loses sight of it. He can put His hand of power on great worlds, and suns, and oceans, and rivers, and winds, and storms, and make them do just what He wishes them to do. And at the same time He makes use of the little rays of light, and the little grains of sand, to work for Him too. What a little thing a drop of water is! How tiny it seems, as it hangs on the tip of your finger! And yet, when God wished to form the mighty ocean, He made use of those tiny little drops for this purpose. What a little thing the pebble stone was that David put into his sling, when he went forth to fight that great giant of Gath! Yet God did more for Israel by that little pebble, than by all the thousands of swords and spears in the army of King Saul. What a little thing a coral insect is! And yet God makes use of that tiny insect to do what all the great whales in the ocean never could do,—build up the coral islands from the bottom of the ocean.

Now let us look at some examples of the way in which God makes use of very little things, to protect, and save His people, when they are in danger; and to comfort them when in trouble.

SAVED FROM DEATH BY FIRE.

Some years ago, a poor old coloured woman lived in the town of West Chester, Chester County, Penn. She was confined to her bed, a helpless cripple. Her home was a little house that stood by itself, where she lived all alone; except that her son, who occasionally came to visit her, would occupy a room in her house for a night. A kind neighbour was in the habit of coming in every day to see her, and to do anything that was necessary to be done. One cold winter's night this neighbour came in as usual. She made everything comfortable in the room, and then left for the night.

About two o'clock in the morning, the old woman awoke, and found that a live coal had fallen from the grate, and had set fire to the rag carpet. It burned slowly on, and came nearer and nearer to the bed. There she lay, without being able to move hand or foot. There was no one near enough, as she supposed, to hear her, if she should call ever so loud. In speaking about it afterwards, she said, "I told the Lord I was quite willing to die; but if He was pleased to let me have my own way, I would rather not be burned to death. And then I waited." The fire gradually crept nearer and nearer. The bedstead was reached, and the bedclothes caught fire. It seemed impossible for her to be saved. But just then the door opened. Her son came in, and she was saved! She did not know that he was in the house. As soon as she was able, she asked how he came there. He said he had returned home late and unexpectedly the night before. Finding her asleep he retired to his room and went to bed. He awoke just then, which he was not in the habit of doing, and fearing he might be late for his work, he came down to his mother's room to see what o'clock it was; and found he was just in time to save her from a dreadful death. He wondered how he happened to wake at that very moment. *But his mother knew who wakened him.*

To wake a man out of sleep is a little thing, yet this

is what Jesus—whose "kingdom ruleth over all," did to save one of His people from a painful death.

Here is another illustration of the same kind.

One of the workmen connected with the railway which runs from Hamburg to Paris, had a good pious wife. When her husband left home one day, to attend to his business, she said, as she was in the habit of doing, "Good-bye. *May God protect you.*" This man was a signal-man. He was stationed at a little watch-house by the roadside. His business was, as the trains came along, to hoist a signal. There were two kinds of signals: one meant—*go on*—when all was right; the other—*stop*—when anything was wrong. On the evening of the day of which we are speaking, he walked along his part of the road, to see that all was right, before the express train came by. Just as he was returning to his watch-house, he was attacked by two bad men who had a grudge against him, and wanted to kill him. They took hold of him; threw him down; bound him hand and foot so that he could not move; and gagged him so that he could not speak. Then they threw him across the rails, and tied him fast, in order that the express train, which was coming along, might pass over him in the dark and crush him. But that gracious Saviour, whose "kingdom ruleth over all," had heard the prayer of this man's good wife—"God protect you," and intended to answer it. Let us see how He did this.

While this horrible thing was taking place on the railway, the wife of the poor signalman was alone in her cottage. All at once, without knowing why, she began to feel very anxious about her husband. She became more and more uneasy, and tried to overcome the feeling; but in vain. At last she said to herself, "I don't know what this means; I never felt so before. Something's the matter with my husband. I must go and see." So she hurried off to the watch-house. She did not walk, but ran, till she reached the place. She hastened down the embankment. She entered the watch-house, but it was empty. Her husband was not there. She was terribly frightened. Where could he be? She called him again and again; but there was no answer. She ran, first to the right, and then to the left, looking for him; but he was not there. What is the matter? Where *can* he be? The train is coming; she hears the whistle of the approaching locomotive, and her husband is not at his post to give the expected signal. Almost wild with terror she hurries back to the watch-house, calling aloud for her husband all the while. Then the thought occurs to her that the signal must be hoisted up, or else her husband will be blamed for neglecting his duty. She hastens to the signal-post, and hoists up a signal. In a few minutes the train comes thundering along; but instead of rushing on, it stands still by the watch-house. She intended to hoist the signal which meant—go on. If she had done so, her husband would have been a dead man in half a minute. But, instead of this, by mistake, she hoisted the signal which said— *stop*. And so the train stopped. It was God who guided her hand. The conductor of the train jumps out, hastens up, and inquires what is the matter. He finds no signal-man at the watch-house, but a weeping woman in great distress because she cannot find her husband. Now lanterns are lighted and they go searching along the road. Soon they find the poor man, bound, gagged, fastened to the rails, and more dead than alive. In an instant he is released and saved. The men who tried to kill him were caught, and punished as they deserved.

If you and I could have gone to that good woman, while she was rejoicing over the wonderful way in which her husband had been saved, and could have asked her what she thought about the kingdom of God? she might well have said—"Oh, it is a beautiful kingdom, because it 'ruleth over all,' and makes the least things, as well as the greatest, work for good to them that love Him."

When that woman went up to the signal-post, it was a little thing whether she pulled one rope or another. But Jesus was there. He overruled that little thing, so as to save the life of that poor man.

And Jesus can overrule little things in the same way *to comfort His people, when they are in trouble,* as well as to save them when in danger.

Here is an illustration that I know to be true, for I am well acquainted with the person to whom it refers.

Some years ago, a young lady from Wilmington, Delaware, went with a sick brother to spend the winter in the state of Georgia. That brother was very dear to her. He had taken his father's place when he died, and for years had been the support, and comfort, and blessing of the family. But now he was attacked with consumption, and the doctor had ordered him to the South, in the hope of saving his life and of restoring him to health again; his sister, accompanied by a faithful man-servant, went with him. For awhile she was cheered by the hope that her brother would get well, and return to bless his household.

But, as the winter passed away, it began to be doubtful whether he would ever get better. And, at last, the doctor told the poor sorrowing sister that her brother never could be well again. And then the painful thought came over her, that her brother had not many days to live; that she must see him die away from her family; that she must bury him there among strangers; and then go back alone to her poor afflicted mother. Her heart sank within her, and she felt unspeakably sad at the thought of having to pass through this bitter trial. At this time, she went one day into the garden, connected with the house where they were staying, that she might be by herself, and think over all her troubles. In a quiet corner of that garden, where no one could see her, she leaned against a tree, and wept in all the sadness of her aching heart. Her brother was dying. Her family were all far, far away. A stranger among strangers, it seemed to her as if there never was any one so sad and lonely as she was. Just then a little piece of paper caught her eye. It was the torn scrap of a newspaper, which the wind seemed to be tossing carelessly about, here and there. Presently another breath of wind caught it, brought it near her, and laid it gently down at her feet. Something prompted her to stoop down and pick it up. She did so, and on turning it over, found these beautiful lines printed on that bit of paper:—

> "*Not all alone:*—the whispering trees,
>   The rippling brook, the starry sky,
> Have each peculiar harmonies
>   To soothe, subdue, and sanctify.
> The low, sweet breath of evening's sigh
>   For thee hath oft a friendly tone;
> To lift thy grateful thoughts on high,
>   To say thou art *not* all alone.
>
> "*Not all alone:*—a watchful eye
>   That notes the wandering sparrow's fall,
> A saving hand is ever nigh,
>   A gracious power attends thy call.
> When sadness holds thy heart in thrall,
>   His tenderest mercy oft is shown;
> Then seek the balm vouchsafed to all,
>   *And thou canst never be alone.*"

These sweet words were a great comfort to that poor, lonely child of sorrow. If an angel from heaven had come down and whispered the words to her she could not have felt more comforted. That scrap of paper, which some one had thrown carelessly away, was a very little thing. And that breath of wind which blew it to her, and laid it down at her feet, was a little thing too. But He whose "kingdom ruleth over all," was pleased to make use of those little things to cheer the heart of His afflicted servant in her loneliness. And when we consider how Jesus can overrule the smallest things as well as the greatest, to help His people in danger, and to comfort them in trouble, we see what beauty there is in His kingdom.

And then there is one other thing that shows the beauty of this kingdom. Jesus not only rules over all the greatest things, and all the smallest things—but He RULES THEM AT ALL TIMES, AND IN ALL PLACES.

Solomon says, "There is a time for everything under the sun." He means by this that there is a particular season when each thing that we have to do must be attended to. If we neglect to attend to it then, it cannot be done at all. For instance, suppose you have a check on a bank for fifty dollars. If you want to get that money you must be sure to go while the bank is open. The banks generally close at three o'clock. If you go there at half-past three, or four o'clock, it will be too late. You cannot get the money then, but will have to wait till the next day. Kings, and rulers, and great men generally, have particular days, or hours, when they can be seen. If you wish them to help you, or to do anything for you, you must go to them at that particular time; or else you will not get the help you want. It is necessary for *men* to have particular hours for attending to business; because they must have time for eating, and sleeping, and resting. And they cannot attend to business when they are eating, and sleeping, and resting. But it is different with Jesus. He never sleeps, and never rests. And the beautiful thing about His kingdom is, that He not only rules over all things —over all the greatest things, and all the smallest things—but He rules them *at all times and in all places.*

His arm never gets weary, and never needs any rest. There are no particular hours of the day in which He attends to His business, as the Ruler of all things. He is attending to it at all times. In summer and in winter, by day and by night, He is always ready to hear, and answer, and help those who call upon Him. He knows what we need before we ask; and He is always waiting and willing to help. Look at yonder sun. It is thousands of years since God made it, and hung it up in the sky. Through all those thousands of years the sun has been shining away as hard as it can. It has never stopped shining for a moment, day or night. And Jesus is just like the sun in this respect. The sun is all the time giving light; and Jesus is all the time governing, and ruling—giving grace, and help, and blessing to His people. Wherever we are, and wherever we go, He is always there beforehand, ready to take care of us and do us good.

The Bible is full of illustrations of the way in which this kingdom is ruling all things, at all times, and in all places. It was this which kept Noah safe while the world was drowning. It was this which kept Lot safe while the storm of fire was burning up Sodom and Gomorrah. It was this which kept Joseph safe, although his brethren had made up their minds to kill him. It was this which kept Moses safe in Egypt, though Pharaoh was very angry with him, and would have killed him if he could. It was this which kept David safe, though Saul was hunting him with an army of three thousand men, all up and down the land, and trying for years to destroy him. It was this which kept Daniel safe in the den of lions, and his three friends when Nebuchadnezzar threw them into the burning fiery furnace. And when Jonah was carried by the great fish down to the lowest depths of the ocean, it was this "kingdom ruling over all," which preserved him there, and brought him safe back to land and to his home again.

And in just the same way this kingdom, as it rules over all things, is preserving people now. Here is an illustration.

Some time ago, a clergyman from New Haven was on a visit to Boston during the winter. He was stopping at the Marlborough Hotel, and was sitting in his room writing a lecture that he was going to deliver. A very severe gale was blowing that day. He stopped in his writing, being at a loss for a word. He clasped his hands over his head, and tilted his chair back, while meditating about the word he wished to make use of. Just while he was doing this, the storm blew down the chimney, and a great mass of bricks and mortar came tearing through the roof and the ceiling, and crushed the table on which he had been writing. If he had not leaned back on his chair *at that very moment*, he would have been killed instantly. The hole made in the roof was from ten to fourteen feet in width. What was it which led this minister to lean back, at that moment, and so to save his life? It was not an accident or chance that happened to him. In a world where God is always present, everywhere, there can be no such thing as accident, or chance. Nothing merely happens. Everything is known, and ordered, or allowed. Jesus, whose "kingdom ruleth over all," was in the room with that minister. It was one of His angels who led him to tip back his chair, and thus to save his life.

And when we think of Jesus as ruling all the greatest things, and all the smallest things, in all places, and at all times, then it may well be said that we are "seeing the King" in the beauty of His kingdom.

If we have Jesus for our friend it will always be a help and comfort to us to think how

"His kingdom ruleth over all."

IV.

THE BEAUTY OF THE KING'S FAMILY.

"THE WHOLE FAMILY IN HEAVEN AND EARTH."
Ephesians iii. **15.**

IV.

THE BEAUTY OF THE KING'S FAMILY.

THE Church of Jesus Christ is compared in the Bible to many different things. At one time it is compared to a city (Isa. xxvi. 1, Matt. v. 14); at another to the moon (Cant. vi. 10); at another to a temple (1 Cor. iii. 16); at another to an olive tree (Hosea xiv. 6). Then it is likened to a vine (Ps. lxxx. 8, 14); to a vineyard (Isa. v. 1–7); to a virgin (2 Cor. xi. 2); to a wife (Rev. xxi. 9); to a mother (Gal. iv. 26). In one place it is compared to a bush on fire (Ex. iii. 2); in another to a garden (Cant. iv. 12, 16); in another to a lily (Cant. ii. 2); in another to a golden candlestick (Rev. i. 20); in another to a flock of sheep (Luke xii. 32); in another place it is compared to a house (Heb. iii. 6); and here, in the words of our text, it is compared to a family. This is one of the most interesting views of the Church of Christ that we find in the Bible. In the family to which we belong we find our home. There we were born and brought up. There we were nursed and taken care of when we were young and helpless. There we were taught when we knew nothing. There we were made acquainted with a mother's tender love and a father's kind and constant care. There we learned to know and love our brothers and sisters. And the brightest hours we have ever spent, and the sweetest joys we have ever known, have been the hours spent and the joys known in the family which makes our home. And so it is pleasant to find that our blessed Saviour speaks of His Church as a family.

In this course of Sermons we are talking about the beauty of Jesus as our King. There are many points of view from which we may look at this beauty. Our present text calls us to consider *the beauty of the King's family*.

This is the subject now before us. The King here referred to is Jesus our Saviour; the family is His Church. And the question we have to try and answer is this—what sort of a family is it of which He is the Head, or King? or what are the things about this family which show the beauty of it? There are four things which show us the beauty of this family.

In the first place, this family of Jesus is—*a* LARGE *family*.

This is one thing that will show its beauty. We think a family is pretty large when there are eight or ten children in it. When the children come to number fifteen or twenty we consider it a *very* large family. But the family of Jesus will be a wonderfully large one. We may judge of the size of this family in part from what the Bible tells us about the home in which they are to live. When Jesus was speaking on this point He said—"In my Father's house are *many* mansions"

(John xiv. 2). By His Father's house here, I suppose our Saviour meant us to understand heaven. And if there are to be "*many* mansions" there, then we may be sure there must be a very large family to occupy all those mansions.

We may form some idea of the many mansions there will be in heaven, from what we read in Rev. xxi. 16. There the heavenly home, or what our Saviour calls our "Father's house," is compared to a beautiful city. The form and size of this heavenly city are very remarkable. We are told that it was, as the apostle saw it coming down from heaven, in the form of a great square city, and each of the four sides of this square city was twelve thousand furlongs in length. Now we know that eight furlongs make a mile. And if we turn these furlongs into miles, which we can easily do by dividing twelve thousand by eight, we get fifteen hundred miles as the length of each of the four sides of this great city. Only think of a city in the form of a square, and with each of its sides *fifteen hundred miles long!* There has never been anything like this in our world. We think that Babylon, of which we read in old times, was a very large city. And so it was. It was built in the form of a square, too, and we are told that each of its sides was fifteen miles long. But each side of this heavenly city is *a hundred times longer* than the side of Babylon was. The city of Boston is about three hundred miles from Philadelphia. If you or I should set off to walk from Philadelphia to Boston, and should walk thirty miles a day, it would take us just ten days to reach there. By the time we arrived we should be ready to think that a city, each of whose four sides was as long as the distance from Philadelphia to Boston, was a wondrously large city. So it would be. And yet, that heavenly city of which the Bible tells us, and which is to be the home of the family of Jesus for ever, is of such a size that each of its four sides is five times as long as the distance between Philadelphia and Boston. If that city had already come down from heaven, as we are told it will do one of these days, and if you and I should start from the corner of one of its jewelled walls, and should travel on foot thirty miles a day, it would take us *fifty days* to walk along one of the sides of that wonderful city.

And then, we are told that that city is to be fifteen hundred miles in *height*, as well as in length and breadth. We cannot tell what to make of such a city as this. Well may the Bible say, as it does, that—"Eye hath not seen, nor ear heard, neither hath entered into the heart," or mind, "of man, the things which God hath prepared for them that love Him" (1 Cor. ii. 9). But this one thing we can all understand very well, that if the city which is to be the home of God's family is so great in its size, then the family which is to occupy that vast home, those many mansions, must be a very large family. When we see what the size of a nest is, we can tell about how large the bird will be that is to occupy that nest. And so when we read about the great size of that heavenly city, which is to be the home of the people of Jesus Christ, we know that the family to be made up of those people must be a very large family.

THE BEAUTY OF THE KING'S FAMILY. 75

Somebody has made a curious calculation to try and find out how many rooms there would be in a city like that spoken of in the Revelation, and how many people could be accommodated there. This would be a pretty hard sum in what is called in our books of arithmetic the cube root. It is too hard for us to attempt to work out here. But we can look, for a moment, at the result which that sum brings before us. In working it out, we may just suppose that each member of Christ's family, in that heavenly city, would have a room for himself to live in, nineteen feet square and sixteen feet high. Then the working out of that sum shows that there would be more than five billions seven hundred and forty-three thousand millions of such rooms in that city. No one can form any idea of such a number as this. Why if our world were to last for a hundred thousand years, and were to have a population of nine hundred millions all the time, and if that population were to die off and be renewed every thirty-three years, and if all those people were to be saved,—yet, at the end of a hundred thousand years, there would not be half enough people to occupy all the rooms in that great city.

But then this is not what the Bible teaches us about heaven. It will not be like a great boarding-house, in which each person will have a room to himself. On the contrary, we are taught to think of it as a beautiful garden, where we are told that Jesus, "the Lamb in the midst of the throne, will feed His people and lead them unto living fountains of water" (Rev. vii. 17). But the size of the heavenly city shows us what a large family our Saviour will have there.

And then the way in which the apostle speaks of this family, in our text, shows us that it must be a large family. He calls it—"*the whole family in heaven and in earth.*" The angels are a part of this family in heaven. We know not how many angels there are. They are spoken of as—"an *innumerable* company of angels" (Heb. xii. 22). We know that there are thousands on thousands of them. How beautiful that family must be which takes in all those holy angels! Then all the dear children who have died, and all the good men and women who have died, and gone to heaven, belong to this family. This is what the hymn means when it says,—

"Angels and living saints and dead
But one communion"—or family—"make."

And when we think of all the angels, and all the good people who have died, from the beginning of the world, and all who are loving Jesus in the world now, and all who shall love Him from now to the end of the world, and all the children who have died in all ages, then we see what a very large family this must be! The members of this family will be gathered out of all countries; they will be of all colours and classes of people, but they will all be made "one in Jesus Christ."

Here is an illustration to show how the members of this family are made alike, though they may come from the opposite ends of the earth.

THE BEAUTY OF THE KING'S FAMILY.

In Whitechapel, London, is a large free day school, connected with one of the churches in that neighbourhood. About eight hundred children attend there every day. These children are very poor. Many of them have no shoes on their feet, and only ragged clothes to wear. But they are interested in the missionary cause, and do something to help it. These poor children subscribe eighty pounds, or four hundred dollars a year, towards a mission school in New Zealand. They are not allowed to give more than a farthing at a time. In this way they support five children in that New Zealand mission school. Those children are clothed, and boarded, and educated by the poor children of the Whitechapel school. These little New Zealanders wear a band over their shoulders, which hangs down in front of them. On the ends of this band are two hearts, worked by the Whitechapel children. In the centre of one heart is marked the word—"Whitechapel;" and in the centre of the other the word—"New Zealand." Across from one heart to the other is a small gold cord, and under it the words—"*Both one in Christ.*"

And so the love that Christians have for their Saviour will make them all one in Him, no matter where they come from. And when we think what a multitude there will be in this family, and every one of them looking as glorious as Jesus looked, when He was on the Mount of Transfiguration, then we see that one thing which has to do with the beauty of this family is that it will be a large family.

*In the next place it will be—*A WEALTHY FAMILY, and this will have a good deal to do with its beauty.

In this world it does not always happen so. Great wealth instead of making people more interesting, or beautiful, often makes them proud, and selfish, and very disagreeable. But it is not so with the family of Jesus. And yet this is the richest family that ever was known. No one can tell how much the members of this family are worth. Generally where a family is considered rich, it is easy enough to tell how much property they own. There are so many houses belonging to them. These are worth so much. They own so much more in different kind of stocks; and then they have so much money in the bank. You can add all these together, and tell how much it amounts to. But if we belong to this heavenly family, then God is our Father. He is very rich. Can anybody tell how much our Father in heaven is worth? We often forget that God is our Father; and how very rich He is.

THE ORPHAN'S FATHER.

Some time ago, a minister was visiting an orphan asylum. The children were seated in a schoolroom, and he stood on a platform. "So this is an orphan asylum," said the minister. "Now, if I should ask if you have a father, many of you would say—No. Would you not?"

"Yes, sir," said several voices.

THE BEAUTY OF THE KING'S FAMILY.

"How many of you say you have no father? Those who say this, please hold up your hands."

A great lot of little hands went up.

"So all of you say you have no father?"

"Yes, sir; yes, sir."

"Now," said the minister, "do you ever say the Lord's prayer? Let me hear you."

The children began: "Our Father, who art in heaven"——

"Stop, children," said the minister, "did you begin right?"

They began again—"Our Father, who art in heaven"——

"Stop again, children," he said. "I hear you all say—'*Our* Father, who art in heaven.' Then you all have a Father in heaven. Let me speak to you a little about Him. He is a good Father,—the best Father in the world. Yes, and He is a very rich Father too. He owns all the gold in California. He owns all the world. He can give you as much of anything as He sees is best for you. Now, children, never forget what a wealthy family you belong to, and what a rich Father you have. Go to Him for all you want, just as if you could see Him. He is able and willing to do all that is for your good."

THE HEAVENLY RICHES.

A Christian lady in England had been very well off; but by some means or other she had lost all her property

She was left so poor that at last she was obliged to go into the almshouse. She was old, and near her end. One day, while a friend was by her side talking to her, he saw her smile and look very happy. He asked her what she was thinking about that seemed to give her so much comfort. "Oh," she said, "I was just thinking what a blessed change it will be, when I go from the poorhouse to heaven. My earthly riches are all gone, but my heavenly riches are all safe. They are the gifts of God in Jesus Christ, and nobody can take them away from me. They will last me for all eternity."

This good old Christian lady was made glad and happy by thinking what a wealthy family she belonged to. And this is the way we ought all to feel, if we are loving and serving Jesus. All things in heaven and in earth belong to Jesus. And all that He has He will share with His people. This is what it means when we are told in one place that we are "*joint heirs with Christ*" (Rom. viii. 17); and in another, that "*all things are yours*" (1 Cor. iii. 21); and in another—"*they shall inherit all things*" (Rev. xxi. 7).

Here is a story that is told of the Apostle Thomas, one of the twelve apostles sent out by our Saviour. I cannot tell you surely that it is a true story; but it comes in very well to show us how we may lay up treasures in heaven, and secure for ourselves a large share of the riches of that wealthy family, to which we belong, if we love Jesus.

The story says that when the Apostle Thomas was preaching in Palestine, our Saviour appeared to him and said, "Leave this country and go to India. Gondoforous the king of the Indies wishes to build a palace finer than that of the Emperor of Rome. Behold now, I send thee to teach him how to build such a palace."

The apostle went. King Gondoforous gave him a very large amount of gold and silver, and commanded him to build for him a magnificent palace. Then the king went into a distant country, and was absent two years. The apostle meanwhile, instead of building a palace, gave away all the money entrusted to him among the poor and the sick. When the king returned and found how his money had been used he was very angry. He commanded the apostle to be seized and cast into prison, intending to put him to death in a very painful way. Just then, the story says that the king's brother died. When they were about to bury him he came to life again. He said to the king—"That man whom you are about to put to death is the servant of God. Behold I have been in Paradise. There the angels showed me a palace of wondrous beauty. It was built out of the gold and silver which that apostle gave away, in your name, among the sick and suffering. Now listen to the teaching of that good man. Love and serve that Saviour of whom he tells, and then that glorious palace will be yours. This is the message I am sent back to bring to you."

Then the king released Thomas out of prison. He listened to his teaching, and was baptized by him, and became a Christian.

Whether this story is true or not, it teaches us a good

lesson. It shows us that the best way of laying treasure *up* in heaven, is by laying it *out* on earth, in doing good with it. And when we think how rich our glorious Saviour is, and how rich He makes all His people who love and serve Him, we see what beauty there is in His family, because it is a wealthy family.

In the third place, this heavenly family is—AN HONOURABLE FAMILY—and this is another thing that shows its beauty.

There are certain things that are considered as honourable in any family. If people can trace their family back a long way, showing it to be an ancient family, *that* is thought to be an honour. If we could trace our family back to that little band of heroic men, the "Pilgrim Fathers," who came over in the "Mayflower," and landed on "Plymouth Rock," we should think that an honour. But if we belong to this heavenly family, let us never forget, that it is the oldest family ever known. Jesus, the Head of this family, is called "*the Ancient of Days.*" "His going forth has been from of old; from everlasting." There is no honour like that of being connected with Him.

THE HIGHEST HONOUR.

Sir Ralph Abercrombie was one of the bravest soldiers that Scotland ever had. He was also an humble, earnest Christian. On one occasion he was elected as an elder in the Presbyterian Church to which he belonged. One of the duties of an elder in

THE BEAUTY OF THE KING'S FAMILY. 83

that Church is, to help the minister in distributing the bread and wine when they celebrate the sacrament of the Lord's Supper.

At the close of the solemn service, in which this brave Christian soldier had been thus engaged for the first time, he asked the privilege of saying a few words, and then turning to the minister, before all the people, he said—

"Sir, I have been honoured by my king with many important and honourable commands during my life as a soldier; and his Majesty has been pleased to reward my services with many most valuable gifts, as tokens of his royal favour; but *this* service, in which I have now been engaged, and have been the humble instrument of putting the emblems of my Saviour's dying love into the hands, even if it were of some of the least of His followers,—this I regard as the highest honour I can receive this side of heaven." Here we see how highly that brave soldier thought of the honour of being connected with this heavenly family!

If we could show that famous princes had belonged to our family, in past years, we should feel that this would help to make our family honourable. But all the members of this heavenly family are called God's princes (Ps. cxiii. 7, 8). And by and by they will all be kings and priests in His glorious presence (1 Pet. ii. 9; Rev. i. 6).

THE HEAVENLY CROWN.

The eldest son of a noble family in Scotland lay on his deathbed. If he had lived he would have succeeded to the dukedom, which belonged to his family. But he was a Christian, and he felt that it was a greater honour to belong to the family of Jesus in heaven, than to be a member of the noblest family in this world. **He** showed this by what he said to his oldest brother when he came to take leave of him. After he had said to him all he had to say about the business of the family, and about his funeral, he ended in these words:

"And now, Douglass, good-bye. In a little while *you* will be a *duke*, but *I* shall be a *king*."

What an honour to belong to a family of which *all* the members will be kings!

If we could show that men famous, not merely for the offices they held but for the noble characters they possessed, had belonged to our family,—men like George Washington of our own country, or John Howard or William Wilberforce of England,—we should feel that it was a great honour to belong to such a family. But in Jesus, the Head of this family, we have the very noblest character that ever was known, either in heaven or on earth; either in this world or in any other. And all the members of His family will be made like Him, in some degree.

Here is an incident which illustrates the noble character of a true Christian.

THE BEAUTY OF THE KING'S FAMILY.

Some years ago, Major Baird, a young officer of the British Army in India, with several of his brother officers, had been taken captive by their enemy, Tippoo Saib. They were thrown into a dungeon. There they had great sufferings to bear. These sufferings were greatly increased by the fact that some of them were severely wounded. One day they were disturbed by hearing the sound of the clanking of iron outside their prison. Presently the massive door of the prison was thrown open, and a party of natives came in, bearing on their shoulders sets of heavy chains. These were flung down on the floor of the dungeon. Then came one of the officers of that cruel tyrant, Tippoo Saib, and gave command that a set of those chains should be fastened on the limbs of each of the captives.

Then they began to fasten the chains on the prisoners. Presently they came to Major Baird. He had been badly wounded. His wounds were still open. One of these was on his leg, just where the iron chain would come. The men are about to put the chain on. A gray-haired English officer steps forward. He is scarred with many an old wound, but still his heart is tender as an infant's. Pointing to the major he says, "Men, for mercy's sake don't do that. You see the wound on his leg. If you put that chain on, it will certainly kill him."

"Kill him or not," says the unfeeling officer, "I can't help it. Here is a set of chains for each prisoner. My order is to see them all put on; and on they must be put."

"Then," says this noble-hearted Christian soldier, "put the major's chains on me, and *let me wear two.*"

Major Baird objected; but his friend insisted, and carried his point. The other set of chains was fastened on him. *He wore two.* Major B. lived to be released from the dungeon, and gain the victory over his cruel enemy, Tippoo Saib. His noble-hearted friend *died in the dungeon.* His name is not known to us; but it is known in heaven, and will be remembered and rewarded there as it deserves to be. "*Let me wear two!*" How truly Christian this was! That was the very spirit of Jesus, who "was made a curse for us," and suffered "the just for the unjust that He might bring us to God." This is the way in which all the followers of Jesus should act. And if all the members of His family try to act in this way—then that heavenly family must be an *honourable* family. This shows the beauty of that family.

There is only one other thing about this family to speak of now as showing its beauty, and that is, it is— a HAPPY *family.*

It is very easy to tell some of the things that will be sure to make a family happy. Suppose, for instance, we see a family all the members of which really love one another. Suppose they show that love by trying to do all sorts of kind and pleasant things to each other; suppose, moreover, that they know they are safe; and are sure of being able to get all that they need to eat, and to drink, and to wear, and to make them comfortable. Well, I think we should expect to find that family a happy family.

Now, if we are true Christians, this is just our condition. We love Jesus, and He commands us to love one another. We must show this love by trying to be gentle, and kind, and pleasant to all about us. We have nothing to be afraid of. Our sins are all pardoned. God is our Father and Friend. He will take care of us. He promises to give us whatever is best for us, while we live in this world; and when we die, He will take us to be with Him, in that blessed home that He is preparing for us. And if we know and believe all this, then we ought to be happy, not only when we are in health and prosperity, but when we are sick and in trouble; not only when we are living, but when we are dying.

Let us look at some examples of persons who were made happy by being members of this family, when nothing else could have made them happy.

REJOICING IN AFFLICTION.

A colporteur in one of our southern cities gives this account of a humble, and afflicted, but happy Christian. "He was an old white-headed negro, known as Uncle Jack. Going in to see him one day, I said—

"'Well, Uncle Jack, how are you?'

"'I's very painful in my knee; but tank my hebenly Master, I've cause to be tankful. My Master jus' gib me 'nuf to make me humble.'

"'And does your religion make you as happy now, Uncle Jack, as it did when you were well, and could go to church, and the meetings?'

"'Yes, massa, I's happier now, and 'joys 'ligion more. Den I trust to de people, to de meetin', to de sarment; and when I hears de hymn sing, and de pray, I feels glad. But all dis ain't like de good Lord in de heart. God's lub yer,'—striking his breast—' make all de hard heart go 'way, and make Jack sit down, and wonder what de good Master gwine to do wid dis yer poor ole sinner.'

"'Then you love God even if He does let you be sick, and in pain?'

"'Oh yes! God—Him do all dis for me good. God wise. Jack don't know. In de night me hear noise. No know what him is; me feel 'fraid. Bime by, morning come. Plenty light den. Me hear noise —not 'fraid den. Me see, me know, me got plenty sense den. Dis life—dark—all same as night. Me no know. But up dare, wid God—all light—me see all— know all den. Glory—hallelujah!'"

Now, certainly *that* was a happy family that Uncle Jack belonged to.

THE HAPPY LITTLE GIRL.

"The happiest child I ever saw," says an English clergyman, "was a little girl I once met when travelling in a railway carriage. We were both going up to London, and we travelled a good many miles together.

She was only eight years old, and was quite blind; had never been able to see at all. She had never once beheld the bright sun, the twinkling stars, the beautiful sky, the grass, the flowers, the trees, the birds, or any of those pleasant things which we see every day of our lives; but still she was quite happy.

"She was all by herself, poor little thing. There was neither father nor mother, relation nor friend, to be with her and take care of her on the journey, and yet she was contented and happy.

"'Tell me,' she said, on getting into the carriage, 'how many people are in this carriage, for I am blind, and can't see anything.' A gentleman asked her 'if she were not afraid?' 'No,' she said, 'I am not afraid. I have travelled before. I trust in God, and know that He will take care of me.'

"But I soon found out why she was so happy. It was because she loved Jesus. I began to talk with her about the Bible, and I was surprised to find how much she knew about it. She talked to me about sin; how it first came into the world, when Adam and Eve ate the forbidden fruit; but how it was to be seen everywhere now!

"Then she talked about Jesus. She told me of the agony in the garden of Gethsemane; of His sweating great drops of blood; of the soldiers nailing Him to the cross; of the spear piercing His side, and the blood and water coming out. 'Oh,' she said, 'how very good it was of Him to die for us; and such a cruel death!'

"I asked her what part of the Bible she liked best. She said she liked all the history of Jesus; but the chapters she most loved to hear were the last two chapters of the Book of the Revelations. I had a pocket Bible with me, so I took it out, and read those chapters to her as we went along.

"When I had done she began to talk about heaven. 'Only think,' she said, 'how nice it will be to be there! *There*, will be no more sorrow, nor crying, nor tears. And then the Lord Jesus will be there; for it says, "The Lamb is the light thereof;" and we shall always be with Him. There will be no night there. But best of all, there will be no blind people in heaven. *I shall see Jesus* there, and all the beautiful things in heaven; won't that be glorious?'"

Now think of this poor little blind girl. Think of her taking such pleasure in talking about Jesus. Think of the joy she felt in hearing the account of heaven, where there is no more sorrow, or night. If belonging to Jesus could make a poor, blind child like this so happy, then the family made up of those who know and love Him must be a happy family.

And the members of this family are happy when they are dying, as well as while they are living. "I hope," said a faithful chaplain to a wounded soldier, who lay upon his cot, in the hospital, with the death drops already gathering on his brow, "I hope you feel happy in thinking of Jesus." "Oh, sir," he replied, "what should I do, if I had not Jesus to trust in now?"

THE BEAUTY OF THE KING'S FAMILY.

The chaplain spoke to another dying soldier. His reply was—"Wrap my blanket around me, and leave me alone with Jesus."

He spoke to a third and asked him if he was ready to go. "Oh yes," said he, "my Saviour in whom I have long trusted is with me now, and His smile lights up the dark valley for me."

And now, let us pass from the hospital, where the soldiers are dying on their humble cots, to the royal palace of England. There Albert the good, the late husband of Queen Victoria, is stretched upon his dying couch. The Queen sits by overwhelmed with grief. The lips of the dying man are moving. Listen to what he says. These are his last words; "I have had wealth, and rank, and power, and I thank God for them; but if these were all, I should *now* be poor indeed!" And then as his spirit was passing peacefully away to its everlasting rest, he whispered these sweet words,

> "Rock of ages, cleft for me,
> Let me hide myself in Thee!"

Yes, that must be a happy family the members of which can find such comfort and joy in the solemn hour of death. And when we think how *large* this family is, how *wealthy*, how *honourable*, and how *happy*, we may understand something about *the beauty of the King's family*.

The words of the Collect, in the Prayer Book, for Christmas Day, are suitable words with which to close this sermon:—"O Almighty God, who hast given thine only begotten Son to take our nature upon Him, and to be born of a pure virgin; grant that *we*, being regenerate and made Thy children by adoption and grace, may daily be renewed by Thy Holy Spirit, through Jesus Christ our Lord. Amen."

V.

THE BEAUTY OF THE KING'S WORK

"HE CRIED WITH A LOUD VOICE, LAZARUS, COME FORTH."—
John xi. 43.

V.

THE BEAUTY OF THE KING'S WORK.

THE RAISING OF LAZARUS.

IF we are walking through a flower garden, it is a pleasant thing to stop and pluck one of the most beautiful of the flowers, and carry it away with us, as a specimen of what is growing there.

When our blessed Saviour was on earth He "went about doing good." This made His life like a garden. The good things that He was doing all the time, are the flowers that grew in this garden. When we read about the life of Jesus in the New Testament, we are walking through this garden. And when we take up one of the wonderful works of Jesus, to examine and study it, we are plucking one of the flowers from this garden. The raising of Lazarus from the grave, after he had been buried four days, was one of the most wonderful things that Jesus ever did. Let us take this now, as a specimen of the beautiful flowers that grew in the garden of our Saviour's life. And when we come to study it, we shall find illustrations in it, of the beauty which marked the way, in which Jesus did His work. It will be like examining a flower, and tracing out its beauty, in the form, or shape, in which it grows; the colours which it puts on, and the sweet fragrance which it gives forth. And in considering the raising of Lazarus there are three things, in the way in which He did it, that illustrate the beauty of the King's work. It may help us in remembering these things, if we bear in mind that each of them begins with the letter P.

In the raising of Lazarus we see the—PITY—*of Jesus in His work.* And this is one thing that shows the beauty of that work.

We read that when He saw the sorrow which the death of Lazarus had wrought upon his sisters, Mary and Martha, "He groaned in spirit, and was troubled." Now it must be so that the more we love a person, the more sorrow we shall feel when we see them in trouble. We are told expressly that Jesus did love this family at Bethany, consisting of Lazarus, and his sisters, Mary and Martha. And when He saw Mary weeping, on account of her dead brother, and the Jews also weeping that were with her, His pity was stirred still more deeply; and we read these two short, but very touching words—"*Jesus wept.*" These are wonderful words. They show us how full of pity, and tenderness, the heart of Jesus is. It was so then, when He was on earth; and it is so now; for He never changes. And when we are in trouble, or sorrow, we may be very sure that Jesus pities us, and feels for us.

And this raising of Lazarus was not the only event in our Saviour's history which showed His pity. His life was full of it. We see it in all His works. When

THE BEAUTY OF THE KING'S WORK.

the blind men came to Him, and asked His help, He pitied them, and opened their eyes. When the lame men came to Him, He pitied them, and gave them power to walk. When the deaf and the dumb came to Him, He pitied them, and unstopped the ears of the deaf, and loosed the tongue of the dumb. When men with withered, palsied limbs came to Him, He pitied them, and showed His pity by telling them to rise and walk, or to stretch forth their useless limbs, and then giving them strength to do so. When Jesus was going by the city of Nain one day, He met a funeral procession. It was the only son of a poor lonely widow woman, whom they were carrying to the grave. The tender heart of Jesus was filled with pity when He saw the distress of that bereaved and heart-broken mother. With what loving tones He said to her, "Weep not!" And then, how quickly He spoke the dead young man back to life, and restored him to the arms of his wondering, but glad and grateful mother!

And, even though the Jews refused to receive Him as their Messiah, and treated Him shamefully, still, when He thought of the miseries which they were thus bringing upon themselves, He pitied them. And one day, when He was walking over the Mount of Olives, which looks directly down upon Jerusalem, we are told that He "beheld the city, and wept over it; saying, O Jerusalem! Jerusalem! how often would I have gathered thy children together, even as a hen gathereth her chickens under her wings, and ye would not!"

And when He hung upon the cross, in all the agony and

pain He was then suffering, He pitied the poor blinded Jews, who were putting Him to death. And He breathed forth the pity of His soul in that wonderful prayer—"Father, forgive them; for they know not what they do."

It is very important for us to know that Jesus has a heart full of tender pity and love.

This is what draws us to Jesus that He may be our Saviour.

"FOR ME."

Little Carrie was a heathen child, about ten years old. She had bright black eyes, curly brown hair, and a neat slender form. After she had been going to the mission school for some time, her teacher noticed one day that she looked sad.

"Carrie, my dear," said the teacher, "why do you look so sad to-day?"

"Because I am thinking."

"What are you thinking about?"

"O teacher! I don't know whether Jesus loves me or not."

"Carrie, did Jesus ever invite little children to come to Him?"

Immediately the little girl repeated this sweet verse she had learned in the school, "Suffer the little children to come unto Me."

"Well, Carrie, for whom did Jesus speak those words?"

In a moment she clapped her hands, and said, "It's not for you, teacher, is it? No; it's for me! it's for me!"

Here we see how the knowledge of the pitying love of Jesus, was just the thing that drew that dear child to Him, for the salvation of her soul. And multitudes have been drawn to Him, in the same way, wherever the Gospel has been preached or taught.

And we need to know the tender pity and love of Jesus, not only that we may trust in Him as our Saviour, but also that we may be encouraged to go to Him for help and comfort in all our troubles.

TELL JESUS.

Here is an illustration from a good Christian woman, in humble circumstances, who was trying to make herself useful.

"On one occasion," she says, "I had been sick a long time. I was unable to work, and my little stock of provisions was exhausted. I had no bread for myself or my children, and no means of getting any. What was I to do? Somewhere my eye rested on the words —'Go and tell Jesus.' I said to myself—'Remember how full of pity He was for the poor and suffering when He was on earth. He is the same in His tenderness now. Go and tell Jesus.'

"I went to my room, knelt down, and told Him all about my trouble, and asked Him to help me, in any way that He thought best.

"I rose from my knees feeling peaceful and happy, and sure that help would come in some way or other. And then I waited to see what God would do for me.

"That very afternoon a man who had never been known to give anything to the poor, drove up to my door and left a sack of flour. And so I knew that Jesus had heard my prayer, and in pity for my distress had sent me what was needed for the wants of my family."

And then we should remember the tenderness and pity of Jesus, not only to encourage us to come to Him ourselves for help and comfort, but also that we may try and be like Him in this respect, when we are working for Him and seeking to do good to others. It is not so much *what* we say or do, as *the way* in which we say or do it, that does people good.

THE POWER OF KIND WORDS.

Some time ago a gentleman in England, who was a Christian, and wished to make himself useful, was in the habit of spending a part of his Sundays in visiting the patients in an hospital near where he lived. He was a man who had learned of Jesus to be kind, and gentle, and loving, in what he said and what he did.

As he went into the hospital, one Sunday, he took his seat by the bedside of a very rough-looking poor man, who had only been brought in the day before. In talking to this man he did not begin at once by telling him that he was a sinner, and in danger of being lost for ever. But, in a kind and tender way, he asked the man some questions about himself—what the sickness was that brought him there, what medicine he was taking, and how long he expected to be in the hospital.

Thus he was trying to get acquainted with the man, and secure his confidence, and then he intended to lead on the conversation to something connected with the Bible, and with Jesus the Friend and Helper of the sick and suffering. But before he had time to get this far he saw that the poor man's feelings were a good deal affected by something or other. His face began to work. His muscles twitched and quivered. At last he lifted up the sheet, and drawing it over his head, he burst into a flood of tears, and sobbed aloud.

The gentleman sat quietly by, and waited patiently till the man got over this feeling. After awhile the poor fellow removed the clothes from over his head. His face was still wet with the tears which had flowed down it. Presently the gentleman said, "I am very sorry, my friend, if I have said anything that hurt your feelings. I assure you I had no intention of doing so. Pray tell me what it was that disturbed you."

As well as the poor man could utter them, he sobbed out these words—

"Sir, you—are—the first man—that—ever—spoke a kind word—to me—since—I was born—and—I can't stand it."

This gentleman had won his way to that man's heart by his tenderness, and then he could do anything with him that he might wish to do.

Now in the raising of Lazarus we see the pity of Jesus. And this is one thing which shows the beauty of His work.

But in the raising of Lazarus we are told of the PRAYER

which Jesus offered. And this is the second thing that shows the beauty of His work.

We read in this chapter how Jesus came with those weeping sisters and their sorrowing friends to the grave in which Lazarus lay dead. It was a cave, and a great stone was over the mouth of it. Jesus told them to take away the stone from the mouth of the grave. This was done. There is the great dark cave in which lies the lifeless body of Lazarus. And now Jesus pauses. Before speaking to the dead man in the grave He lifts up His eyes to heaven, and speaks to His Father there. We call this a prayer that Jesus offered. You will find it in the 41st and 42d verses of this 11th chapter. But it is a very remarkable prayer. It is rather a thanksgiving than a prayer. In our prayers we always ask God to do something for us, or give something to us. But we find nothing of this kind here. Jesus does not ask the Father in heaven to raise Lazarus from the dead, nor to help Him to do it. He just thanks God for always hearing Him. He speaks to Him just as you or I would speak to a dear friend, who was always with us; to whom we told all our secrets; and with whom we shared all our thoughts and plans and pleasures. Jesus seems to have offered this prayer, or thanksgiving, or whatever we call it, on purpose to show to His disciples, and to the Jews, and to all His people, how entirely united He and His Father in heaven were. They always thought, and felt, and acted as much alike as if they were one person. They are two persons indeed, and yet they are but one God. Jesus was able to do

THE BEAUTY OF THE KING'S WORK.   103

anything that He wanted to do. And yet, when He was going to do anything important, He always prayed to His Father in heaven. Before He ordained His twelve apostles, and sent them out to preach the Gospel, He spent the whole night in prayer. And before He went to meet the great sufferings that were awaiting Him in Gethsemane, and on Calvary, He offered that beautiful prayer, more for His people than for Himself, that we find written in the 17th chapter of St. John. Jesus prayed, in connection with the work He did, not so much for His own sake, as to teach us, by His example, how to do the work we have to do, and to bear the trials that God puts upon us. When we have hard work to do, and heavy burdens to bear, there is nothing like prayer to make that work easy and those burdens light. Let us look at some illustrations of the way in which great good has been done by prayer.

LIFE SAVED BY PRAYER.

There is a good man in the city of Philadelphia who is a bishop in the Methodist Church, a man well known and greatly beloved. I refer to Bishop Simpson. Some years ago a Conference of the Methodist Church was held in Indiana. It was presided over by Bishop Janes. During the meeting of that Conference, Bishop Janes received a telegram telling him that Bishop Simpson was very ill and not expected to live. He read this telegram to the Conference, and then proposed that they should pause in their business and unite together in prayer to God, that it might please Him to spare the life of Bishop Simpson. They did so. Very earnest prayers were offered, with many tears, that this valuable life might be spared.

When they rose from their knees one of the ministers present said to another—

"Bishop Simpson will not die."

"Why do you think so?"

"Because I had this feeling very strongly impressed on my mind while we were praying for him."

Bishop Simpson did not die. The minister just referred to wrote down in his note-book the day and the hour when that meeting for prayer was held. The first time he met Bishop Simpson, he said to him, "Bishop, how did you recover from that last sickness?"

"I can't tell."

"What did the doctor say?"

"He said, it seemed like a miracle."

"Can you tell me the day and hour, Bishop, when the change took place?"

He mentioned the time. It corresponded exactly to the time when the Conference were praying for his recovery. "As the doctor then left my room," said the Bishop, "he told my wife that nothing more could be done for me. I must die.

"In about an hour he returned; feeling my pulse he started back and asked—'What have you been doing?'

"'Nothing,' was the reply.

"'Why, he is getting better,' said the doctor. 'A

change has taken place in the disease within the last hour such as I never knew before. The danger is over. The Bishop will get well.'" And so he did. He was saved by the prayers of his friends a thousand miles away. And if prayer has such power as this, it was a beautiful thing in the work of Jesus that when raising Lazarus from the grave He prayed Himself, so as to encourage us to pray.

Here is another example. We may call it—

GETTING OUT OF TROUBLE BY PRAYER.

A German minister, who lived in the Black Forest, had a good Christian wife who was remarkable for her strong faith in God. She believed in the power of prayer, and two striking anecdotes are mentioned in her life of the way in which she got out of trouble by prayer.

She and her husband had six children, whom they were trying to educate; but, as they had very little money, they found it hard, at times, to meet their expenses. Connected with the parsonage in which they lived were some acres of land, which they carefully cultivated. They depended on the sale of the crops from this land, to help them in educating their children.

One summer, just before the harvest time, heavy clouds were seen gathering in the sky, and rolling over the valley in which they lived. Presently a violent hail-storm burst forth at a distance, and began to sweep up the valley. On it went, destroying the crops wherever it came. The pastor's wife went to her room and engaged in earnest prayer. She told God how much they were dependent on the harvest for the support of their children, and entreated Him to save their crops from being destroyed. Then she waited calmly to see what would come of her prayers.

When the storm was over they went out to see what the effect of it had been. Wherever the storm had reached, the crops were entirely destroyed. But the pastor's crops were uninjured. The prayers of his wife had been heard and answered. Just as the storm reached the parsonage land, an unseen hand had stopped its progress, and turned it aside in another direction. Somebody has said that "Prayer moves the arm that rules the world." This is very true. We see it illustrated in this case.

But here is another illustration of the power of prayer in the life of this same good Christian woman.

One day her husband received three letters. Each of these letter contained a bill for the education of one of their three boys, who were at school at a neighbouring town. The letters said the bills must be paid promptly, or else the boys would be sent home. They had no money with which to pay these bills. The husband was in great distress. He had not as much faith in God as his wife had. He said they would be ruined. She said, "Let us have faith in God, and pray to Him for help."

"Faith and prayer are very well in their place," said he, "but they will not do to pay bills with."

At the close of the day his wife took the bills, and

went up to a little private room of her own, and locked herself in. Then she knelt down and spread out those bills before God. She told Him of their trouble. She spent a good part of the night there in earnest prayer, that God would in some way send them the money they so much needed.

When she had done praying, she went downstairs, feeling perfectly comfortable in her mind, and quite sure they would be helped.

While they were at breakfast the next morning, a message came that a Christian friend of theirs in the village, and who was very rich, wished to see the pastor's wife. She went to see him. He met her warmly and said, "I'm very glad you have come." Then he led her into the parlour, and said, "I cannot tell why, but I could not sleep any last night for thinking of you. For some time I have had several hundred golden guilders lying in that chest (a golden guilder is a German coin worth about two dollars of our money), and all night long I was haunted by the thought that you needed this money, and that I ought to give it to you. If this be so, then there it is, take it by all means; and don't trouble yourself about paying it back. If you are ever able to make it up again, well and good; if not, never mind."

"Yes, my kind friend," said the pastor's wife, "I do most certainly need it. Yesterday three letters came, telling us that our three boys would be sent home unless the bills for their boarding were paid at once. We had nothing to pay them with, and I spent the greater part of the night praying to God for help."

"Is that so?" asked her astonished friend. "How strange and wonderful! Now I am doubly glad that I asked you to come."

Then she went home with the golden guilders. How astonished her husband was when she laid them down on the table. And then he learned this lesson, that faith and prayer while good for other things, are also good sometimes for paying bills. And when we think of the prayer of Jesus at the grave of Lazarus, we see the beauty of His work.

But in raising Lazarus we see the POWER *of Jesus.* And this is the third thing that shows the beauty of His work.

Jesus did many things while He was on earth which showed His power, but nothing did this more than the raising of Lazarus. When He opened the eyes of the blind, when He cleansed the lepers, and healed the sick, and cast out devils, He was showing His power. When He walked upon the sea as on dry land, and when He hushed the angry storm to instant stillness by a word, He was showing His great power. But the raising of Lazarus showed His power more than anything else He ever did while He was on earth. Lazarus had been dead four days. For four days his body had been as cold as marble; for four days the blood in his veins had stopped flowing; for four days the heart had ceased its beatings, and had been still; for four days his spirit had left the body, and had been in that unseen world, where the souls of men go to when they die. But when Jesus stood by the open mouth of that dark grave and cried out—"Lazarus, come forth," all that death had

THE BEAUTY OF THE KING'S WORK. 109

done to that buried man was undone in a moment. The cold body grew warm. The blood in his veins, that had dried up and stopped flowing, became liquid and began to flow again. The still, quiet heart, which had ceased its beating, and had been standing still for four days, began to beat once more. And the spirit of Lazarus, away off in the world of spirits, heard the call of Jesus. In a moment it came flying back, and once more entered that dead body, which had so long been its home before. And Jesus did all this by His own power.

When the prophet Elijah wished to raise the widow woman's dead son to life again, he knelt down and prayed, saying, "O Lord my God, I pray Thee let this child's soul come into him again." But when Jesus wished to raise His dead friend Lazarus to life, He had only to speak and it was done. The voice of Jesus had power to do all that He wished to have done. And the power that Jesus has, makes the work that He does seem beautiful.

The last time I came from England I was a passenger on board the steamer "Scotia" of the Cunard Line. During that voyage I remember going one day, with my good friend Dr. S. A. Clarke, now in heaven, down into the engine-room to see the machinery which moved that huge vessel through the water. It was a very interesting sight. There was that vast engine. It seemed like a giant in iron, doing its work steadily but quietly. The different parts of that huge machinery were all busy. The crank that turned the great iron shaft, to which the paddle-wheels were fastened, was of a prodigious size. It seemed to me as if there were a mountain of iron in that crank alone. And yet, notwithstanding its vast size, it kept going round and round as smoothly and as easily as the tiniest wheel of a watch. It was a beautiful thing to see an engine at work that had so much power in it. And after that, when I lay in my berth at night, it was a comfort to think of that engine. I wanted to get home again, and I felt sure that as that engine kept on working, and that great crank going round and round, there was power enough in it, by God's blessing, to bring me "to the haven where I would be."

And so we may feel, when we think of standing by the grave of Lazarus, and there seeing the power which Jesus had to bring the dead man back to life. If Jesus could do *that*, He can do anything. He said, "*All power is given unto me in heaven and on earth.*" It is a comfort to know this. Jesus is working with this power all the time for the good of His people. And this power enables Him to do anything for us that He wishes to have done. Let us look at one or two examples of the way in which He uses this power.

HELPED THROUGH A DREAM.

The late Rev. Dr. Bushnell, a well-known minister of New England, used to tell this story about a remarkable dream, and said he knew the story to be true. He had a friend living in the Far West, who had been for many years, like Nimrod, "a mighty hunter." His name was Captain Young. He was a kind of patriarch among the hunters in that part of the country. He was well known, and was greatly loved and respected.

One night the old hunter had a strange dream. He dreamed that he saw a company of emigrants overtaken by a snow storm in crossing the Rocky Mountains, and perishing from cold and hunger. He had so clear and distinct a view in his dream, of the place where these people were, that he could have drawn a picture of it when he awoke. One thing that he saw in his dream made a particular impression on his mind; this was a tall, perpendicular cliff of white rock that lifted itself up into the sky near where these people were, and which had a very peculiar appearance. In his dream he saw the men cutting off what appeared to be the tops of trees, and struggling to get out of the deep gulf of snow. He saw the very looks of the persons in the snow, and noticed what great distress they seemed to be in. When he awoke he was greatly surprised. It seemed so much like a real scene he had been looking at, that he could hardly believe it was only a dream.

Presently he fell asleep and dreamed the same dream over again, precisely as he had seen it before. In the morning he could think of nothing else but this strange dream.

Going out after breakfast he met an old friend, who like himself had been a hunter in former days, and was well acquainted with the pass, across the mountains, known as the "Carson Valley Pass." He told him about his dream, and described what he had seen in the dream, and especially the tall, perpendicular white rock. His friend told him that he recognised the place from his description of it, and then told him in what part of the pass he would find that singular looking rock. Captain Young was a Christian man. He believed what the Bible teaches about the providence of God. He felt satisfied that there were some people up among the mountains in distress, and that this was the means God was using to have help sent to them. He began at once to collect a company of men, and to send them up into the mountains with mules, and blankets, and necessary provisions. His neighbours laughed at him. "Laugh away," he said, "as much as you please. I am able to do this; I have made up my mind to do it, and I will do it, for I am sure this dream comes from God."

The men were sent into the mountains a hundred and fifty miles distant, directly in the heart of the Carson Valley Pass. There they found scenery answering to what the captain had beheld in his dream. The tall, perpendicular white rock was there, and there they found a company of travellers overwhelmed by the snow, just as the captain had seen in his dream. Some of them had already perished, but the rest were relieved and brought safely back by the help the good captain had been led to send them, in consequence of that remarkable dream. Jesus has power to work in this way, and this power makes His work seem beautiful.

We have one more illustration of the way in which Jesus can use His power, in order to protect and take care of those who trust in Him. This event occurred, too, in our great western country. We may call it

GOD'S PRESERVING POWER.

This incident took place several years ago. It shows how wonderfully God protected the life of a little girl only nine years old, from the fierce wolves of the forest. The parents of this child are named Sutherland. They live in Platteville, Colorado. The story about this child was published in the "Denver News" of November 29th, 1875.

This little girl went with her father one cold afternoon to the woods to find the cattle and bring them home. They had not gone very far when they found the calves; but the cows were not with them. They had wandered farther away. So her father told the little girl to follow the calves home, while he went on to hunt up the cows. She did so, but the calves misled her, going off in a different direction; and before long the child found that she had missed her way and was lost in the forest. Soon night came on, a cold November night, and the hungry wolves were heard growling savagely around. With strange calmness the poor child kept walking slowly on and on all through the night, not knowing where she was going. The next day, which was Sunday, about ten o'clock in the morning, she reached in her wanderings the house of John Beebe, near a place called Evans, having travelled on for eighteen hours, and a distance of not less than twenty-five miles. When she was missed at home all the neighbours turned out to hunt for her, but in vain. There was great rejoicing in that neighbourhood, when she was brought safely back. Many questions were asked her about how she got through the night. In answer to these " she said that the wolves kept close to her heels, and snapped at her feet; but her mother had told her that if she prayed to God and trusted in Him, He would always take care of her, and so she knew the wolves wouldn't hurt her, *because God wouldn't let them.*" God wouldn't let them! Blessed, believing child! Sweet, precious faith! How I wish that you, and I, and all of us, had just such faith in God as this dear child had! Here we have the story of Daniel over again, in our own day and country. The God of Daniel has the same power now that He had then. And if we only had the faith of Daniel, and the faith of this dear child, we should have more of this power put forth for our help and deliverance.

And when we think of Jesus raising Lazarus from the dead, we see three things that show us the beauty of His work. These are—the *pity*—the *prayer*—and the *power* —of Jesus. Let us learn to pity those in trouble, as Jesus pitied them. Let us pray for them as Jesus prayed. And though we cannot exercise the same power that He exercised in doing our work, yet we may be sure that that power will help us, and will protect and bless us, as we work for Him. And so we may well say that in the raising of Lazarus we see

THE BEAUTY OF THE KING'S WORK.

"She knew the wolves wouldn't hurt her, because God wouldn't let them."

VI.

THE BEAUTY OF THE KING'S WORK.

"I AM THE RESURRECTION."—*John xi.* 25.

VI.

THE BEAUTY OF THE KING'S WORK.

THE GENERAL RESURRECTION.

THESE words, "I am the resurrection," were spoken by Jesus to Martha, the sister of Lazarus, whom Jesus loved. He generally made His home at their house in Bethlehem, when He was at Jerusalem. Lazarus was dead, and had been buried four days before. But Jesus was going to raise him from the dead. How He did this we saw in our last sermon. And now He wished to comfort Martha, by telling her that He had the power to raise the dead. This was what He meant when He said, "I am the Resurrection." The resurrection means, raising the dead to life again. Jesus wished Martha to know that He had the power to do this. And He proved the truth of what He said directly after. For He went with the weeping sisters, Martha and Mary, to the grave of their dead brother. "It was a cave and a stone lay upon it. Jesus said, Take ye away the stone." Some of the men rolled it away. There is the open cave. We can look in and see the dead man lying there. The Jews did not use coffins, as we do. They simply wrapped their dead in grave-clothes. Jesus stands by the open grave and says, in a loud voice, "Lazarus, come forth!" And in a moment the dead man starts into life, and walks forth from the grave. How well Jesus might say, "*I am the Resurrection.*"

And He was not only the resurrection to others, as to Lazarus, to the daughter of Jairus, and to the widow's son at Nain, but He was the resurrection to Himself also. He said to the Jews, when speaking of His own life, "No man taketh it from me, but I lay it down of myself. I have power to lay it down; and I have power to take it again" (John x. 18). And so, though after He had been put to death on the cross, and was buried, death could not keep Him. On the morning of the third day, He restored Himself to life. He rose from the dead by His own power. He was the resurrection to Himself. He came forth from the grave to die no more. As the apostle says, "Death hath no more dominion over Him." And, from the very earliest times, large portions of the Christian Church have kept Easter Sunday, as a glad festival in memory of the resurrection of Jesus. And we may very well rejoice when we think that Jesus has risen from the dead. For if Jesus had not risen, we should never rise. But when Jesus rose from the dead, and came forth from the grave, He proved that He had power to raise you, and me, and all of us, from the grave. And this is what He meant when He said, "I am the Resurrection." He intended we should learn from this, that He has the power which is necessary to enable Him to raise all the dead to life again, and that He will do this when the time comes that God has fixed for it. Every grave will one day be opened, and every dead person be made alive again. What Jesus wants us to know is, that He has the power to do this. And this is what He teaches us when He says, "*I am the Resurrection.*" And so we may well say, in the language of the Apostles' Creed, "*I believe in the resurrection of the dead.*"

In this sermon we are called upon to look at the beauty of the King's work, as it is seen in the resurrection.

It is not the resurrection of Jesus that we are now to speak about, but our own resurrection, the resurrection of all people, or as we say, the *general resurrection.*

There are *two thoughts* about the resurrection to be remembered; and *two lessons* from it to be learned: and in both of these we shall see the beauty of the King's work.

The thoughts and the lessons of the resurrection.

The first thought to be remembered in connection with the resurrection is—that it is VERY CERTAIN.

And there are two things which show how certain it is. One of these is what God teaches us about it *outside of the Bible;* and the other what He teaches us about it *inside of the Bible.* Outside of the Bible God speaks to us and teaches us many important things. The world of nature around us, is like a great book, in which God is speaking to us all the time. And there are many things here that seem to speak to us of the resurrection.

DAY *and* NIGHT *speak to us about it.* When evening

comes, and the sun sets in the west, then it may be said that the day dies. Night is the grave in which the day is buried. And when the sun rises again in the morning, it is the resurrection of the day.

And then *the* SEASONS *of the year speak to us about the resurrection.* In spring-time the year is young. In summer the year is of age. In autumn the year grows old. In winter it dies. Winter is the grave in which the year is buried. And when spring comes back again, it brings the resurrection of the year. Then the trees begin to bud and put forth their fresh leaves, "the flowers appear upon the earth, the time for the singing of birds is come, and the voice of the turtle-dove is heard in the land." And in all these things, God speaks to us about the resurrection.

The INSECTS *speak to us about the resurrection.* Here is a caterpillar. He spends his days in going about as a creeping thing. But when he comes to be an old caterpillar, and his crawling days are over, he weaves for himself a cocoon, which is like a little coffin. Then he lies down to take a long sleep. It seems as if he were dead. He remains there awhile, like a body that has been buried in the grave. But after a long time has passed by, that coffin opens, and the worm, or caterpillar, that seemed to be dead, comes out from its little coffin wondrously changed. It is turned into a butterfly. And no king upon his throne was ever so beautifully dressed as he is now. Look at his wings. Did you ever see such brilliant colours? How they glitter in golden glories as he flits about in the beams of the sun! And so, every butterfly that we see in the bright summer days, is a little minister that God sends to preach to us about the resurrection.

The FROGS *speak to us on this subject.* Suppose we make a visit to a frog pond. There are plenty of frogs in it, and we hear them, in different keys, uttering their hoarse, loud sounds, and singing bass. This is the part they take in the great hymn which nature is always singing to the glory of God. When winter comes they disappear. But they cannot fly away, as the birds do, to find a warmer climate till the cold weather is over. And so, in His goodness, God provides them with convenient and comfortable winter quarters, in the pond where they live. They go down to the bottom of the pond and bury themselves in the mud. There they remain without either sense or feeling. It seems like sleep, or more like death, only they do not decay as dead things do. In this state they remain all winter. And now spring returns. The weather grows pleasant again. Some mild day in early spring we have a warm rain, and there is thunder with the rain. As the loud peals of thunder are heard sounding through the sky, like the archangel's trumpet of the last day, they wake up the frogs from their death-like sleep, and then the croaking for another season begins again. And so, when we hear the familiar sounds they make, we may well say that God is making use of the hoarse voices of the frogs, to speak to us of the resurrection.

These are some of the ways in which God speaks to us about the resurrection outside of the Bible.

But it is *in the Bible* that He speaks most plainly to us on this subject. Nothing in the world is more certain than that Jesus rose from the dead. But God tells us that it is just as certain *we* shall rise from the dead, as it is that Jesus did rise. If you wish to read what God says on this subject, you will find it in the fifteenth chapter of First Corinthians, from the 20th to the 22d verse: "Now is Christ risen from the dead, and become the first-fruits of them that slept. For since by man came death, by man came also the resurrection of the dead. For as in Adam all die, *even so in Christ shall all be made alive.*" When it says here, that "all shall be made alive," it means that all shall be raised from the dead. This makes the resurrection certain. This is enough to settle the matter, if there was nothing else in the Bible about it. But there is something else. There is one passage in which Jesus Himself speaks of it. His words are so clear, and so strong, that they should remove all doubt about the resurrection. I refer now to John v. 28. Here Jesus said, "Verily, verily, I say unto you, that the hour is coming in which *all that are in their graves shall hear the voice of the Son of Man, and shall come forth.*" This makes it so sure that nothing more need be said on this point.

The other thought about the resurrection is, that it will be VERY WONDERFUL.

There will be many wonders about the resurrection. The change itself of a dead thing, no matter what it is, to a live one, must always be wonderful. Here, for example, is a walking-stick. It is dead and dry. These little marks upon it show where branches were growing on it when it was alive. Now suppose, as I hold it in my hand, this dead stick should come to life again. Suppose that each of these places where the branches used to be, should swell out, and bud, and put forth leaves, and that the bark should begin to grow over the outside of this cane, and roots should spring out from the bottom of it, and from being a dead stick it should become, at once, a live young tree. How very wonderful this would be! Or, suppose that you and I are walking together in a cemetery. We come to an open grave. We stand at the edge of the grave and look down. There is a coffin at the bottom of the grave. It was put there many years ago. The lid of the coffin has been taken off. The body in the coffin has turned to dust. Only the bones of the skeleton remain. There they lie in the coffin just as they were left when the mouldering flesh fell from them. Every bone is in its place. But they are all loose. There is nothing to hold them together. But, suppose that while we are looking at it, the sinews, or strings, that once bound those bones together, should come back and bind them to each other again. And then suppose, that we should see the flesh begin to grow all over those bones. Then the skin comes and covers the flesh. The hair grows out on the head. The mouth, the nose, the ears, the eyes, are in their proper places. And inside the body is the breast, with all its wonderful contrivances. It begins to beat again. The lungs begin to breathe. The bosom rises and falls. The paleness of death leaves the cheeks and the rosy hue of health takes its place. The eyes open. The man rises to his feet and leaps out of the grave, a strong, hearty, living man! How very wonderful this would be! To see *one* such change as this would be wonderful. But at the time of the resurrection there will be not one nor a few such changes, but hundreds, and thousands, and millions of them. Every grave in all our crowded cemeteries will be opened then. No matter where any body has been buried, or whether it has been buried at all, it must rise from the dead. How many persons have been drowned in the depths of the sea! How many have been burned by fire, or devoured by wild beasts! It makes no difference. God knows where to find all that belongs to every particular body, and how to make it alive again. It was easy for Him to make our bodies out of nothing, in the beginning; and it will be easier for Him to make them all out of something, when He wants to do so. And when we think of this great change taking place in such multitudes of cases, we see how very wonderful the resurrection will be.

And then, the resurrection will be very wonderful, too, in the way of doing it. Some people are not willing to believe in the resurrection, because, they say, it is a thing too hard to be done. Now, if you or I had to do it—if all the men in the world or all the angels in heaven had to do it—this would be a good reason for not believing it. It would be too hard for us and too hard for them. But the resurrection will be the work of God, and not of men or angels. The *power of God* is that by which it is to be done. And we know that "nothing is too hard for the Lord." "All things are possible with Him." Whatever He desires to do, He can easily do; and when He begins this work of the resurrection it will not take Him long. The Apostle Paul tells us that it will be done "*in a moment, in the twinkling of an eye*" (1 Cor. xv. 52). When God made the world it was done at His word. "*God said, Let there be light, and there was light*" (Gen. i. 3). David says, "*He spake, and it was done; He commanded, and it stood fast*" (Ps. xxxiii. 9). And *so*, we are told, He will do this great work of the resurrection. God will send an archangel from heaven to sound a trumpet; and while that trumpet is sounding, the voice of God will be heard speaking to all that are in their graves. "They will hear that voice and will come forth." As St. Paul says, "*The trumpet shall sound and the dead shall be raised.*" As Jesus stood by the grave of Lazarus and called him back to life, so it will be just as if He were standing by your grave, and my grave, and every grave, calling each one by name, to come out from the grave. And every one called will come forth. How wonderful this will be!

And then the resurrection will be wonderful in the BEAUTY *that will mark the bodies of those who are raised.* I cannot tell anything about the bodies of those who are not Christians. But, if we love Jesus, I can tell just how *our* bodies will look when they rise from the grave. Suppose that you and I were standing on the top of Mount Tabor, if that was the place, where Jesus was transfigured. Moses and Elijah have come down from heaven on a visit to Him. Look, there is Jesus, sitting on that rock. And see what a change is taking place in His appearance! His clothing becomes as white as snow, whiter than anybody on earth could make it. His face becomes bright and shining like the sun, only still more glorious! And this is the pattern according to which our bodies will be made at the resurrection, for the apostle says He will "*change our vile bodies, and make them like unto His own glorious body*" (Phil. iii. 25). And in another place we are told that "when He shall appear, *we shall be like Him*" (1 John iii. 2). I suppose our bodies will be in size, and shape, and general appearance, very much like what they are now, so that we shall know one another as easily as we now do; only all imperfections will be removed, and they will be made to look perfectly glorious. Suppose you have the image of a little man made of iron, or clay, and suppose this image were changed to silver, or gold. You could tell it in a moment, as soon as you saw it. And you would be ready to say, "Why, only look; here's my old clay image turned to gold! How beautiful it looks!" And when we think how changed our bodies will be at the resurrection, when we think what multitudes of these bodies there will be, when we think of the wonderful way in which this change will be brought about, and of the great beauty that will mark them, we may well see—how wonderful the resurrection will be!

These are the two *thoughts* we should remember when we think about the resurrection: it is *very certain ;* and it will be *very wonderful.* And here we see the beauty of the King's work.

And now we come to speak of the resurrection as showing the beauty of the King's work, *in the* LESSONS *that it teaches us.*

There are two lessons taught us by the resurrection, that we should try to learn and practice.

These are the two most important lessons we shall ever have to learn. And they are lessons we should begin to learn now, while we are young.

One lesson is—HOW TO LIVE.

We cannot understand what God has put us in this world for, and how He wants us to live here, till we learn about Jesus and the Resurrection.

THE FINAL EXAMINATION.

You know that the United States' Government has a large Military Academy at West Point, on the North River. There the officers for the army receive their education. The course of study they have to pass through is long, and very severe. When they have finished their studies, before leaving the academy, the students, or *cadets,* as they are called, all have to pass through a last examination. That examination is to decide the rank, or honour, they are to have in graduating. And every good student feels anxious about that examination. If he shall pass that examination well, he will take a high and honourable position as he goes out in life. If he shall fail in his examination, it will be a disgrace to him that he will hardly ever get over.

A young man who was a student at West Point, some time ago, had been preparing for this examination with great care. He had been head of his class all through the academy. He wished to pass such an examination that he might graduate at the head of his class. He was so anxious and excited about it, that when the examination began, and the first question was asked him, he fainted and fell senseless on the floor.

That young man had been thinking about this last examination all the time he was in the academy. He was trying every day to be such a good student that he might be sure to pass a successful examination at last. And he did so. The thought of that examination taught him how to live as a student.

And this is the lesson we should learn from thinking about the resurrection. Immediately after the resurrection will come the last judgment. That will be our great examination. If we pass that examination well, we shall have honour and happiness for ever. If we fail, then we shall be lost for ever. It is only by loving, and serving, and believing in Jesus, that we can pass safely through the last judgment. But nothing will help us to do this so well as understanding and believing what the Bible teaches about the resurrection.

We have all heard about the great good that was done in England, Scotland, and Ireland, through God's blessing on the labours of those two earnest Christian men from America, Messrs. Moody and Sankey. Here is a story connected with their work that illustrates this point of our subject. We may call it—

THE GIPSY FORTUNE-TELLER.

Some young men who had been converted through the preaching of Mr. Moody, wished to try and do some good themselves ; and in the hope of being useful to others, they began to hold religious meetings, in which they read the Scriptures, and talked to the people of " Jesus and the resurrection." A band of gipsies was strolling through that part of the country. A woman belonging to this band attended one of these meetings. There she heard, for the first time in her life, what the Bible teaches about the resurrection. God blessed what she heard to the good of her soul. She was led to repent of her sins, and became a humble believer in Jesus. And so, thinking about the resurrection taught her how to live.

Not long after this, several wild young men, who wanted to have some sport, visited the gipsies' encampment. They happened to come to this woman who had become a Christian, and asked her if she could tell them their fortunes. She said she could, and invited them into her tent; " for," said she, " I have the best fortune-telling book in the world."

Then opening her basket, in which she had formerly kept her charms and books, that pretended to tell the meanings of dreams and such things, she took out a New Testament. Opening this book, she turned to the last verse of the third chapter of St. John's Gospel, and read these words :

"He that believeth on the Son of God hath everlasting life; and he that believeth not the Son hath not life, but the wrath of God abideth on him."

"There, my friends," she added, "that is what God says about your fortunes; and you may be very sure that every word of it is true."

The young men were greatly surprised. This was a kind of fortune-telling that they had not expected. They went away from the gipsy's tent, but they could not go away from the words of God, which the gipsy woman had spoken to them. Those words became the power of God to their salvation. From being wild, thoughtless young men, they became humble, earnest Christians.

Mr. Moffatt, the celebrated missionary to Southern Africa, tells a very good story of the effect produced on the mind of an African chief, when he first heard the missionary preach about this great Bible doctrine of the resurrection. It illustrates this part of our subject very strikingly.

Mr. Moffatt was making a long journey into the interior of Africa, hundreds of miles away from his own station. In the course of his journey he wished to visit a famous chief named Macaba, who was a great warrior. He had fought many battles and killed multitudes of people. He was the terror of all his enemies. Some people in the neighbouring tribes tried to persuade Mr. Moffatt not to visit this chief. They said he was risking his life in going there. But the missionary trusted in God and went. Macaba received him very kindly and asked a great many questions about the religion of Jesus.

One day Mr. Moffatt went by special request, or invitation, to have a great "palaver," as they call it there, or a talk with this man of war and bloodshed. He found him waiting for him, with fifty or sixty of his head men and warriors seated around him.

On this occasion the missionary talked to the chief about the resurrection, and told him what the Bible teaches us on this subject.

After listening for a while, the chief started with surprise, and exclaimed—

"What! what are these words about the dead? The dead—the dead arise, did you say?"

"Yes," said the missionary, "*all* the dead will arise."

"Will my father arise?"

"Yes," said the missionary.

"Will all that have been killed and eaten by lions, and tigers, and crocodiles, arise?"

"Yes; and come to judgment."

Turning to his warriors, the chief shouted, "Hark, ye wise men, did your ears ever hear such strange words as these?"

Then, turning to the oldest man among them, who was considered the wise man of their tribe, he asked, "Did *you* ever hear such news as this?"

"Never," said the old man; "I thought I knew a good deal: that I had all the knowledge of the ancients:

but these words are too much for me. This man must have lived before our oldest men were born!"

Then the frightened chief laid his hand on the shoulder of the missionary and said, "Father, I love you much. Your visit has made my heart white like milk. The words of your mouth are sweet like honey; but these words of a resurrection must not be spoken again. I do not wish to hear any more about the dead rising. The dead cannot rise. The dead shall *not* rise."

"Tell me, my friend," said the missionary, "why I must not speak of the resurrection."

Lifting his arm which had been strong in battle, and shaking his hand as if grasping a spear, the chief said, "I have slain thousands and they *must not* rise again."

You see, this heathen man felt that he could not go on fighting and killing men, and living as he had been doing, if he believed in the resurrection. If this was true, he knew that he would have to live a different life. And so it will be with us. If we understand what the Bible teaches us about the resurrection, and really believe it in our hearts, one lesson that it will teach us is —*how to live.*

The other lesson it will teach us is—HOW TO DIE.

There are many things in this world that are very uncertain; but *this* is not one of them. Whatever else we are not sure about, we may be *very sure* about this. We *must* die. *I* must die. *You* must die. *All* of us must die. We can get rid of some things: but we cannot get rid of this. And if this is so, then the most

important lesson in the world for us to learn is this—
how to die. I mean by this, how to die without being
afraid of death : how to die a happy death.

Now the Bible speaks of death as having a *sting.* This
sting is sin. But when Jesus pardons our sins, this sting
is taken away. Then death becomes a harmless thing,
and there is no reason why we should be afraid of it.
Then it is true, as the hymn says, that—

> "Death is but the servant Jesus sends
> To call us to His arms."

This idea, that death is the servant of Jesus, was very
sweetly expressed, in different language, by a Christian
woman who was suddenly taken very ill, and was just
about to die.

"You are dying," said a friend who was with her.
"Shall I not send for a clergyman to come and pray
with you ?"

"Oh no ; never mind," she said, "I am ready to die
at any moment."

"But are you not afraid to die ?"

"No," she said very cheerfully, "I am not afraid ; for
I belong to death's Master. I am a sinner saved by
grace, a child of the resurrection."

And when we love Jesus, and understand and believe
what the Bible teaches about Him and the resurrection,
then we may well say that we "belong to death's
Master." There is nothing in death for us to be afraid
of.

Here are two boys who are going to dive into the

water, but under very different circumstances. One of them is standing on a rock that overlooks the ocean. The water beneath him is rough and dark. He knows nothing about this water into which he has to dive. He cannot tell how deep this water is, nor what danger there may be in it. He has heard about sharp, jagged rocks in the sea, and dangerous whirlpools, and horrible monsters, ready to eat up whatever comes in their way. Whether any of these things are in the water before him he cannot tell. They may be all there. When he dives into this water he cannot tell what may happen to him; or whether he will ever come up out of the water again. And under these circumstances we do not wonder to find that the boy is not willing to dive. He shrinks back at the thought of the unknown dangers that may lie hid under that dark water.

This illustrates what death is to those who do not love Jesus, or know about the resurrection.

And now let us look at the other boy. He is going to dive into a pond in his father's meadow. He knows that his father had the pond made. He knows just how deep it is. He knows that there are no rocks, or whirlpools, or horrible monsters, or dangers of any kind in that pond. He knows perfectly well that when he dives into that water, he will only remain a little while under it; and then he will come up again, all safe and sound. We do not wonder that *this* boy is not afraid to dive. And this illustrates what death is to us when we love Jesus, and believe what the Bible tells us about the resurrection.

Then we can very well say in the words of the hymn—

> "I would not live alway; no, welcome the tomb;
> Since Jesus hath lain there, I dread not its gloom:
> There sweet be my rest, till He bid me arise,
> To hail Him in triumph descending the skies."

And so we see that when we understand and believe what Jesus teaches us about the resurrection, it will teach us—*how to die.*

BABY, COME FORTH.

A little child was taken once to the funeral of one of his young companions. He had never seen a dead body before. He looked long and earnestly on the beautiful form of his little friend as it lay, like a piece of waxwork, or of polished marble, in the dark coffin, with flowers all over it. He did not go to the cemetery. His mother took him, and let him stand at the window, where he could see the funeral procession of his playmate go by. He looked at it with fixed attention for awhile. Then he turned to his mother, and his face lighted up with gladness as he said—

"O mamma! how beautiful it will be when Jesus says, *Baby, come forth!*"

The little fellow was thinking, no doubt, of what he had heard about Jesus standing by the grave of His friend, in Bethany, when He said—"Lazarus, come forth!"

That dear child was making the right use of what the Bible teaches us about Jesus and the resurrection. In the morning of the resurrection, Jesus will speak, in that way, to all the dead children, and to all His people, who died believing on Him. And it will indeed "*be beautiful when they come forth!*"

"*WE'LL ALL MEET AGAIN IN THE MORNING.*"

A little child, who had been taught about Jesus, was dying. It was at the close of a bright summer day. The sun was setting and his red rays were shining through the window, on the bed where he lay. The child's mother had died some time before. His father sat weeping by the bedside of his darling child. Stretching out his hand the little one said—

"Good-bye, papa; mamma has come for me to-night. Don't cry, papa, *we'll all meet again in the morning!*"

How sweet this was! Here we see that what this dear child had learned about the resurrection had taught it *how to die.*

The resurrection will come like the morning, after a long, dark night. And then, if we love and serve Jesus here, we shall "all meet together in the morning." A beautiful and blessed meeting that will be!

Jesus said, "I am the Resurrection."

Remember the two thoughts about the resurrection—*very certain,* and *very wonderful;* and the two lessons—*how to live,* and *how to die.*

Let us try to remember these two thoughts, and learn these two lessons, and then we shall see the beauty of the King's work in the resurrection, and shall be making a right use of it.

VII

THE BEAUTY OF THE KING'S LESSONS.

"WHAT TIME I AM AFRAID I WILL TRUST IN THEE."
Psalm lvi. 3.

VII.

THE BEAUTY OF THE KING'S LESSONS.

THE LESSON OF TRUST.

PERHAPS some of you may think that grown-up men ought never to be afraid. But this is a mistake. Strong men, and good, and wise, and brave, are sometimes afraid; yes, and they have reason to be afraid. David was a man when he wrote this psalm. He was a strong man, a wise, a good, and brave man. He was a great king and a great soldier. He had fought many great battles, and gained many great victories. When he was only a boy he was not afraid to go alone and fight with the wild beasts—the lion and the bear—that stole away the lambs from his flocks. And when the great Philistine giant, Goliath, came to defy the army of Israel and challenged any of their soldiers to come and fight with him, the bravest among them were afraid of him, and were ready to run away as soon as they saw him. But David was not afraid of him. Although he was only a lad and had never been in a battle, yet he went bravely out, all by himself, without a sword, without a shield, or spear, or a bit of armour on, and with nothing in his hand but his sling and his stone, he fought with that great monster of a man. David was a very brave man. And yet he was not ashamed to speak about the times when he felt afraid. And if this was so with David, it may well be so with us. We need not be ashamed to say that there are times when we are afraid. The one great thing that makes people afraid is—sin. Sin and fear always go together. If we were not sinners we never should be afraid. The good angels are not afraid, because they have never sinned. Adam and Eve never knew what fear was till after they had sinned. But then, as soon as they heard God speaking to them, "they hid themselves among the trees of the garden, *because they were afraid.*" And so, if we did not know that we were sinners, we should have nothing to fear. It is only sin that makes us afraid. But, because we are sinners, there are many times when we are afraid. Some persons are afraid to be alone; afraid to be in the dark; afraid when it thunders; afraid when they are sick; afraid when they are in a storm at sea; and afraid when they are going to die. David speaks here of the times when he was afraid, but he does not tell us what those times were. Yet he shows us here how to get rid of our fear, or what to do when we are afraid. He says—"*What time I am afraid I will trust in Thee.*"

The subject which this text brings before us is—*The lesson of trust.* It is one of the lessons we are taught by Jesus our King; and we may see the King's beauty in the lessons that He teaches.

But before going any further let me say that these

THE BEAUTY OF THE KING'S LESSONS.

words only refer to those who are true Christians, or who are really trying to love and serve God. We have no right to trust in God till we are sorry for our sins, and believe in Jesus, and are trying to please Him. Then, indeed, what time we are afraid, we may trust in God.

I wish to speak of three things that may help us to learn this lesson of trust when we are afraid. Each of these three things begins with the letter P; and so it may help us to remember this sermon if we think of the three P's.

And the first thing that should lead us to trust in God when we are afraid is—the thought of His PRESENCE.

But the thought of God's presence affects different people in different ways. If we do not love God, and are not trying to serve Him, it will not comfort us to think about Him. I suppose it was when David was living in sin that he said, "I *remembered God* and was *troubled.*" When we know that we are doing wrong we want to get away from God, or to forget all about Him.

I remember hearing of a girl who went into a room belonging to the gentleman for whom she worked—a room that was not often used—in order to steal something. Hanging over the mantel was a portrait of the gentleman's father. The girl looked at this portrait, and its eyes seemed to be gazing at her. Whatever part of the room she went to, those eyes followed her. She felt uncomfortable. "I can't steal while those eyes are looking right straight at me," she said to herself.

Then she got a chair, and took a pair of scissors, and bored out the eyes of the portrait. And when she felt that she was rid of those troublesome eyes, she went on to steal as she wished to do. But she forgot that God's eyes were looking at her, and that she never could put them out.

That is the way the thought of God makes us feel when we are doing wrong. But when we love God, and feel that He is our best friend, then the thought of His presence always gives us comfort and takes away our fear.

GOD'S PRESENCE A COMFORT IN BANISHMENT.

A company of good Christian people had once been sentenced to banishment on account of their religion. They were to be sent away to a wild and desolate part of the country. As they were passing out from the place where they had lived, some persons were standing by looking at them. One of these said to a friend standing near—

"I pity these poor people very much. They have to leave home behind them, with all its comforts, and go to live in such a barren and desolate place."

"That is true," said his friend, "but you forget one thing. These good people will have God's presence with them, and that will be better than home and any society they could have there. God will go with them, and His presence will be the best comfort."

This is just what good John Newton thought, when

he wrote that hymn about God's presence, in which he says:

> "While blest with a sense of His love,
> A palace a toy would appear;
> And prisons would palaces prove,
> If Jesus would dwell with me there."

TRUST IN GOD.

"Mother," said a little girl, "what did David mean when he said, 'Preserve me, O God, for in Thee do I put my trust'?"

"Do you remember," said her mother, "the little girl we saw walking with her father in the woods yesterday?"

"Oh yes, mother, wasn't she beautiful?"

"She was a gentle, loving little thing, and her father was very kind to her. Do you remember what she said when they came to the narrow bridge over the brook?"

"I don't like to think about that bridge, mother; it makes me giddy. Don't you think it is very dangerous —just those two loose planks laid across, and no railing? If she had stepped a little on either side, she would have fallen into the water."

"Do you remember what she said?" asked the mother.

"Yes, ma. She stopped a minute, as if she was afraid to go over, and then looked up into her father's face, and asked him to take hold of her hand, and said,

'You will take hold of me, dear father; I don't feel afraid when you have hold of my hand.' And her father looked so lovingly upon her, and took tight hold of her hand, as if she were very precious to him."

"Well, my child," said the mother, "I think David felt just like that little girl, when he wrote the words you have asked me about."

"Was David going over a bridge, mother?"

"Not such a bridge as the one we saw in the woods; but he had come to some difficult place in his life, there was some trouble before him that made him feel afraid; and he looked up to God, just as that little girl looked to her father, and said, 'Preserve me, O God, for in Thee do I put my trust.' It is just as if he had said, 'Please take care of me, my kind heavenly Father; I do not feel afraid when Thou art with me and taking hold of my hand.'"

And here we see what David means in our text when he says—"What time I am afraid, I will trust in Thee." The thought of God's presence took away his fear and gave him comfort. This helped him to learn the lesson of trust.

A BOY'S FAITH.

Two little boys were talking together about a lesson they had been receiving from their grandmother on the subject of Elijah's going to heaven in the chariot of fire. "I say, Charley," said George, "but wouldn't you be afraid to ride in such a chariot?"

"Why, no," said Charley, "I shouldn't be afraid, if *I knew that the Lord was driving.*"

And that was just the way David felt when he said —"What time I am afraid, I will trust in Thee." He knew that neither chariots of fire, nor anything else, could hurt him, if God was present as his protector and friend.

COMFORT IN GOD'S PRESENCE.

A ship was once tossing on the stormy sea. She had sprung a leak. It was impossible to stop the leak, and the angry waves were dashing over her deck. The captain said it was not possible to keep the ship afloat much longer, and their only hope of safety was to get into the life-boat. But that tiny little thing seemed only like a nutshell, as it was tossed about by the angry sea. Many stout hearts were afraid when they thought of trusting themselves to that frail boat. Yet there was no help for it.

One of the first who ventured into the boat, as it rose and fell beside the sinking ship, was a delicate woman with a babe in her arms, and a little boy clinging to her dress. The great billows tossed the little boat about, just as you would toss a ball. A gentleman was the next to get into the boat. As he took his seat beside the little boy, who neither cried nor spoke, he said, "Aren't you afraid, my child, to be in such a storm?"

"I don't like the storm, sir," he replied, "but mother is here, and I'm not afraid where mother is;" and he clung closer to her side.

"And are you not afraid, madam?" said the gentleman to the mother.

She shook her head, and pointing upwards she said, in a voice that could hardly be heard amidst the roaring of the storm, "God is ruling the storm, sir. He is my Father and my best Friend. I know He is here, and I am not afraid of anything where He is present."

That was just what David meant when he said, "What time I am afraid, I will trust in Thee." He felt that the thought of God's presence was enough to take away all his fear.

The gentleman in the boat was surprised at that mother's trust in God, and to see how it took away her fear. But he was not a Christian. He could not look up to God as his Father and Friend; and the thought of His presence gave him no comfort. The little boat got safe to land, but the gentleman never forgot that Christian mother's words of trust, spoken in the time of fearful danger. "What time I am afraid, I will trust in Thee." The first thing that should lead us to learn this lesson of trust is *the thought of God's presence.*

The second thing that should lead us to learn this lesson is the thought of God's POWER.

The Bible teaches us that "power belongeth unto God" (Ps. lxii. 11). And it invites us to have confidence in God for this very reason. It says, "Trust ye in the Lord for ever, for in the Lord Jehovah is everlasting strength" (Isa. xxvi. 4). God can do

BEAUTY OF THE KING'S LESSONS.

anything that He pleases. Nothing is hard or impossible for Him to do. When He made this great and beautiful world, He just *said* how He wanted things to be, and they came out exactly so. The Bible tells us that—"He spake, and it was done; He commanded, and it stood fast" (Ps. xxxiii. 9). When He wanted to have light, He said—"Let there be light; and there was light" (Gen. i. 3). And when He wanted to drown the world for its wickedness, He told the waters to come; and they came. And all the people in the world could neither stop them from coming, nor get out of their way when they came. And if this God is our Friend, it will be a great comfort when we are in danger to think of Him. The thought of His power may well lead us to trust Him when we are afraid.

Suppose we go and stand upon a rock by the seashore where the waves are dashing up. How strong that rock seems! The waves roll up and break in foam upon it, but they can neither move it, nor shake it. And if we look at the rock when the waves roll back and leave it bare, we shall find a number of tiny little shell-fish clinging to the sides of the rock. These are very weak. They have no power at all to resist the waves that dash against the rock. If they were left to themselves, the first wave that came would sweep them all away. But God has given them the tiniest little sort of fingers with which they can take fast hold of the rock. And when the great rolling waves come up, and sweep over the rock, they cling to its side and are safe.

And God's power is to us just what that rock is to the little shell-fish. And our faith in God is just like those little fingers by which the shell-fish cling to the rock. And so when we are afraid, the thought of God's power should lead us to trust in Him.

A gentleman was walking down a street one morning when he saw a little blind boy standing on the sidewalk, with his head bent forward as if listening for something. Stepping up to him he said,

"Shall I help you across the street, my little friend?"

"Oh no, thank you, sir; I'm waiting for my father."

"Can you trust your father?"

"Oh yes; my father always takes good care of me. He leads me all the time, and when he has hold of my hand I feel perfectly safe."

"But why do you feel safe?"

"Raising his sightless eyes, with a sweet smile and a look of perfect trust, the dear boy said, "Oh, sir, because my father knows the way. I am blind, but he can see. I am weak, but he is strong."

And this is just the kind of feeling we should have towards God. *He knows the way, and He is strong.* The thought of His power should lead us to trust Him, when we are afraid.

A good woman was visiting among the poor, in London, one cold winter's day. She was trying to open

BEAUTY OF THE KING'S LESSONS.

the door of a third-story room in a wretched-looking house, when she heard a little voice inside say, "Pull the string up high! Pull the string up high!" She looked up and saw a string. She pulled it, when it lifted the latch, and the door opened into a room where she found two little half-naked children all alone. They looked cold and hungry.

"Do you take care of yourselves, little ones?" said the good woman.

"No, ma'am, God takes care of us," replied the elder of the children.

"You have no fire on this cold day. Are you not very cold?"

"Oh! when we are very cold we creep under the quilt, and I put my arms round Tommy, and Tommy puts his arms round me, and we say, 'Now I lay me,' and then we get warm," said the little girl.

"And what do you have to eat, pray?" asked the visitor.

"When granny comes home she fetches us something. Granny says we are God's sparrows, and He has enough for us. And so we say 'Our Father' and 'daily bread' every day. God is our Father."

Tears came into the eyes of this good woman. She had sometimes felt afraid that she might be left to starve; but these two little "sparrows," perched alone in that cold upper room, taught her a sweet lesson of trust in the power of God which she felt that she should not soon forget.

PERFECT TRUST.

A gentleman was walking one evening, with his little girl, upon a high bank, beneath which ran a canal. The child was pleased with the look of the glistening water, and coaxed her father to take her down to it.

"The water looks so pretty. Please, papa, do take me down there," she said.

The bank was very steep and the road a mere sheep path. In getting down the gentleman had to take hold of his little girl's arms and swing her from point to point. While doing this she would sometimes be hanging in the air, directly over the water. Yet she only laughed and chuckled, but was not the least bit afraid, although she really seemed to be in great danger.

At last they got down the bank and reached the towpath in safety. Then taking up his daughter in his arms he said, "Now tell me, Sophy, why you were not afraid when you were swinging in the air, right over the water?"

Nestling her plump little cheek upon her father's face, she said—

"Papa had hold of Sophy's hand; Sophy couldn't fall!"

This was very sweet. Here was a perfect trust. And this is just the feeling that David had towards God when he said, "What time I am afraid, I will trust in Thee." Sophy would have screamed with terror to find herself hanging over the water in the canal, unless she had confidence in the person who had hold of her arms. But it was her father—her kind, loving father—who held her, and so, "what time she would have been afraid she trusted in him." And this is the feeling that we ought to have towards God. The thought of His power should lead us to trust in Him.

THE ANXIOUS AMBASSADOR.

There is a good story told of an English ambassador that illustrates this part of our subject very well. It took place more than two hundred years ago, during the time of Oliver Cromwell. That was a period of revolution and war and of great trouble in England. The gentleman, to whom I refer, had been appointed ambassador to the court of Sweden. He had reached a seaport town from which he was to sail the next morning. He expected to be absent from his country for some time, and things were in such an unsettled state that he felt very much distressed at the idea of being away. He kept thinking about the country, and was so much troubled that he couldn't sleep. He had a servant with him, who was a good Christian man, and had learned well this lesson of trust. He was sorry to see his master so worried and troubled about the country. So he came to him and said, "Please, sir, will you allow me to ask you one or two questions?"

"Certainly," said the ambassador.

"Well, sir, don't you think that God governed the world very well before you came into it?"

"Undoubtedly He did."

"And don't you think He will be able to govern it quite as well when you are taken out of it?"

"Certainly He will."

"Then, sir, please excuse me, but don't you think you may as well trust Him to govern it while you are in it?"

To this he could give no answer. But it had a good effect upon him. It showed him the folly of trying to take the government out of God's hands. He quit worrying. He cast away his fear. He trusted the country to God, and went quietly to sleep.

Just one other short illustration on this point.

THE LOST BOY'S TRUST.

A little boy and his brother were lost in a western forest. After being out a day and a night they were found. In giving an account of what took place while they were in the woods, the little fellow said:

"When it got dark I knelt down and asked God to take care of little Jimmy and me, *and then we went to sleep!*"

How simple, how beautiful that was! That little boy was feeling, and acting, just as King David did when he said—"I will both lay me down in peace and sleep; for Thou, Lord, only makest me to dwell in safety." And so from all these examples, we see that the second thing which should lead us to learn the lesson of trust in God, is the thought of His power.

BEAUTY OF THE KING'S LESSONS. 153

The third thing that should lead us to learn this lesson is the thought of God's PROMISES.

God's promises are given to us on purpose to help us in trying to learn this lesson of trust. These promises are made to apply to all the times and circumstances, in which we are most likely to be afraid. Sometimes we are afraid that our strength will fail, and that we shall not be able to do what we have to do. And then God gives us this sweet promise: "Fear not, I am with thee; I will strengthen thee; yea, I will help thee; yea, I will uphold thee, with the right hand of my righteousness" (Isaiah xli. 10.) Sometimes, we are afraid of the anger and violence of wicked men, and then God says to us, as He did to His servant Abraham of old, "Fear not, I am thy shield, and thy exceeding great reward" (Gen. xv. 1). Sometimes, we are afraid of the troubles and afflictions we may have to meet, as we go on in life; and then God gives us this precious promise, "When thou passest through the waters I will be with thee; and through the rivers they shall not overflow thee; when thou walkest through the fire, thou shalt not be burned; neither shall the flame kindle upon thee" (Isaiah xliii. 2). The waters and the fires spoken of here, mean trials and afflictions; but if God is only with us we need not be afraid of them. Sometimes, when we think of dying, and of going above into an unknown world, we feel afraid, and our hearts sink within us. But, even when we think of meeting death, we may take up the language of David, and say—"Yea, though we walk through the valley of the shadow of death we will fear no evil; for Thou art with us; Thy rod and Thy staff they comfort us" (Ps. xxiii. 4). God promises to "make all things work together for good to them that love Him" (Rom. viii. 28). And all these promises are given to teach us the lesson of trust when we are afraid.

A CHILD'S TRUST IN GOD'S PROMISES.

Here is a story of a poor little German boy who had learned this lesson of trust, from God's promises in the Bible. He wanted to enter the Moravian school to get an education; but his widowed mother was too poor to send him. So he wrote a letter, and directed it thus—"To the Lord Jesus Christ—in heaven"—and dropped it into the post-office. The letter ran thus:—

"MY LORD AND SAVIOUR, JESUS CHRIST:

"I have lost my father, and we are very poor. But Thou hast promised, in Thy word, that whatsoever we shall ask of God, in Thy name, He will give it to us. I believe what Thou sayest, Lord. I ask then, in the name of Jesus, that God will give my mother the money to send me to the Moravian school. I should like so much to go on with my learning. I pray unto Thee already; but I will love Thee more."

The postmaster was very much surprised at the direction on the letter. He knew that the mail had no connection with that country, and that it was impossible to send the letter to heaven; so he opened it, and read it. He gave it to a member of the Moravian Church. It was read at a meeting of their society. A rich lady present was so much interested in it, that she took charge of the little boy, and sent him to school as he desired.

FAITH IN PROMISES.

There was a captive once brought before a prince in Asia. He had been condemned to death for some offence, and was about to be beheaded in the presence of the prince. He had bowed his head, and the glittering sword was already lifted up to strike it off. But he was suffering dreadfully from thirst. He raised his head and asked for a drink of water. A cupful was handed him; he held it as if afraid that the sword would fall while he was drinking it. "Don't be afraid," said the prince, "your life will be spared till you drink that water." Trusting to that promise of the prince he instantly dashed the cup of water to the ground. The faith of the poor man, in the promise of the prince, saved his life. The prince would not break his promise, and the man was allowed to go on his way rejoicing.

TRUST IN A PROMISE.

A little girl whose mother had always told her the truth, and taught her to trust in her promises, went with her one day to a large town. The child had been used to live in the quiet country, and the noise and bustle of the city were not pleasant to her. A great crowd was gathered to see some show in the street, and Lucy pressed her mother's hand, for she felt afraid. "Don't be afraid, my child," said her mother. "I won't take you into any danger. Keep hold of my hand, and nothing will hurt you." Lucy believed her mother, and was happy.

After awhile it began to rain. The mother looked at her delicate little girl and said, "Lucy, dear, I am afraid to take you any farther on account of the rain. I have some business in another part of the town. I must leave you in this store. Don't go away from it, and I will come for you as soon as I get through my errands." The child looked into her mother's face and said, "You won't forget me, I know."

Then her mother kissed her, and left her under the care of the storekeeper.

At first she was amused by seeing the gay ribbons measured, and in watching the ladies who came in to do their shopping; but after awhile she grew tired, and wished for her mother to come. Then, a little girl older than herself came in, and they began to talk together. Lucy told her she was waiting for her mother, who had promised to come for her when she got through her errands.

"Aren't you afraid your mother may forget you?" asked the little girl.

"No, I'm not afraid. I'm sure she won't do that," said Lucy.

"How can you be sure? She *may*, you know."

"She *promised*," was the child's reply, "and I never knew my mother break her promise."

Another hour passed away. How long it seemed to Lucy! The customers had all gone home. The people in the store were putting away their goods. It was growing dark, and the gas lamps were lighted, but still her mother did not come. A lady came into the store whom Lucy knew. She lived near her father's house, and offered to take her home in her carriage.

"No, thank you, ma'am," said Lucy, "mother said she would come for me, and I know she will keep her promise."

At length her mother came. How glad Lucy was to see her! And when they were sitting by the fireside, in the evening, her mother told her this was just the kind of trust that God wanted His children to exercise. He gives us promises in His Word, and expects us to believe them, just as we believe the promises of our parents and dear friends. "What time we are afraid" we must trust in His promise, and then we shall find comfort. The great promise of God in the Gospel is, "Whosoever believeth shall not perish." The way to be saved is—just to trust in this promise with all our hearts. Then we need never be afraid about getting to heaven.

I have just one more illustration of the way in which the remembrance of God's promises should help us to learn the lesson of trust in Him, when we are afraid.

A CHILD'S FAITH.

Johnny Hall was a poor boy. His mother worked hard for their daily bread. "Please give me something to eat, for I am very hungry," he said to her one evening. His mother let the work that she was sewing fall upon her knees and drew Johnny towards her. As she kissed him the tears fell fast on his face, while she said, "Johnny, my dear, I have not a penny in the world. There is not a morsel of bread in the house, and I cannot give you any supper to-night."

Johnny didn't cry when he heard this. He was but a little fellow, but he had learned the lesson of trust in God's promises. He had great faith in the sweet words of Jesus when He said, "Whatsoever ye shall ask the Father in my name, He will do it."

"Never mind, mamma, I shall soon be asleep, and then I sha'n't feel hungry. But you must sit here and sew, hungry and cold. Poor mamma!" he said, as he threw his arms round her neck and kissed her many times to comfort her.

Then he knelt down by his mother's side, to say his prayers after her. They said "Our Father" till they came to the petition, "Give us this day our daily bread." The way in which his mother said these words made Johnny's heart ache. He stopped and looked at her, and repeated them with his eyes full of tears—"Give us this day our daily bread." When they got through he looked at his mother and said, "Now, mother, don't be afraid. We shall never be hungry any more. God *is* our Father. He has promised to hear us, and *I am sure He will.*"

Then he went to bed. Before midnight he woke up, while his mother was still at work, and asked if the bread had come yet. She said, "No, but I am sure it will come."

In the morning, before Johnny was awake, a gentleman called, who wanted his mother to come to his house and take charge of his two motherless children. She agreed to go. He left some money with her. She went out at once to buy some things for breakfast. And when Johnny awoke, the bread was there, and all that he needed. Johnny is a man now; but he has never wanted bread from that day; and whenever he was afraid, since then, he has remembered God's promises and trusted in Him.

Let us remember these three P's, the *presence*, the *power*, and the *promises* of God, and this will help us to learn the lesson of trust. And in all our times of danger and of trial, let us try to follow the example of David, when he said—

"What time I am afraid, I will trust in Thee."

VIII.

THE BEAUTY OF THE KING'S LESSONS.

"A SOFT ANSWER TURNETH AWAY WRATH."—*Proverbs* xv. 1.

VIII.

THE BEAUTY OF THE KING'S LESSONS.

THE LESSON OF GENTLENESS.

If you look at a house or barn in the country, or some of the larger buildings in a city, you will often find an iron rod stretching up above the highest point, and then running down along the side of the building, into the ground. We call these lightning rods. They are very useful. In summer, when sudden storms arise, and the lightning flashes, large buildings are in great danger. If they are not provided with these rods the lightning, as it darts forth, will sometimes strike them. If they are wooden buildings they may be set on fire and burned down. If the buildings are of brick or stone they are sometimes rent and shattered, and greatly injured. The persons who are in a building when it is struck by lightning are often injured, and sometimes killed. But a lightning rod will protect a building from this danger. It lifts its pointed finger into the air, sometimes with a single point, at other times with several points; and when the lightning flashes out, this rod will attract it. And then, instead of striking the building and tearing it to pieces, the lightning, like a ball of fire, runs quietly along the iron rod down into the ground, and does no harm. This is the way in which the lightning rod protects a building from danger during a storm.

But anger or wrath is like a storm. And the sharp, cross words, which persons speak when angry, are like the lightning that flashes out from the dark storm-cloud, as it passes over us. These angry words strike the hearts of those to whom they are spoken as the lightning strikes a building, and do much harm. But "a soft answer," says Solomon, "turneth away wrath." Such an answer is like a lightning rod. As that rod turns away the lightning from the bursting storm, and prevents it from doing injury, so the kind words of a gentle, loving person turn away the wrath of an angry man, and prevent the evil that would follow.

By the "soft answer" here spoken of, is meant kind and gentle words. Solomon was not speaking for himself, but for our blessed Saviour. We may regard this text as teaching us one of His lessons. It is—*The lesson of gentleness.* And there are *three great things* in gentleness. As we look at these we shall see *the beauty of the King's lesson.* And the thought of this beauty, should lead us to learn and practice this lesson.

The first great thing that we find in gentleness is—*Great Power.*

This shows us the beauty of the King's lesson.

The greatest powers that we find in nature do their work in the quietest and gentlest way. There is the sun, for instance. He has great power and is using it

BEAUTY OF THE KING'S LESSONS.

all the time. Why, if all the steam engines in the world could be made to work together, they would not have half as much power as the sun has; and yet the very smallest of those engines makes a great deal more noise than the sun does. You know how quietly the sun rises in the morning; how quietly he shines all the day; and then, when evening comes, how quietly and gently he sinks behind the western hills! And real gentleness is like the sun in this respect, it has great power, but uses it in a quiet way.

Anger or wrath is a powerful thing. If you storm at it, and use violence, you never can manage it. That is like going against the tide, or flying in the face of the whirlwind. It only leads to trouble. But, when gentleness meets wrath or anger with its kind words and soft answer, the anger is conquered or turned away. Let us see how this is done.

A good Christian man was very much disliked by some of his neighbours, on account of his religion. They hired a man named John to strike him whenever he passed by him. Meeting this good man in the street, not long after, John struck him a hard blow. The man turned round and quietly said, "May God bless you, my friend." This was not what John expected. If the man had turned round and stormed at him, or called him hard names, he would not have minded it. *Then* he would have been willing to go on hitting him whenever he had a chance. But that "soft answer," those gentle words, he could not stand, he took the money back to the persons who had hired him and said,

"Here, take your money. I wouldn't strike that man again for the world."

And this was not the end of it either. John was so convinced that there was something more in this man's religion, than he knew about, that he was led to pray earnestly to God, and finally he became a Christian himself. Here we see what great power there is in gentleness.

THE POWER OF LOVE.

A kind Christian lady, on a visit of charity, met with a poor little orphan girl, who had neither home nor friends. She brought her to her own home. But, finding herself among strangers, the poor child felt very unhappy. She sat in the hall of her kind friend's house, weeping. This lady had three young daughters. They tried to make friends with the little stranger; but she was timid and frightened, and turned shrinkingly away from them.

"There is a secret," said this kind mother, "which will act like a charm on this poor child. It will draw her to you, and make her willing to go anywhere with you. This secret lies in a word of four letters. Now see if you can find it out, my darlings."

Then the children began to think what this secret could be. They looked among their prettiest playthings to find something that would answer. At last the oldest daughter said—"I know what it is; D-o-l-l is a word of four letters. I'll try my pretty new doll." So she took her best doll and offered to give it to the child if she would come into the parlour. But this had no effect upon her.

Then the next in age said to herself, "M-u-f-f is a word of four letters. Perhaps this is it." So she took her beautiful muff, that was given her at Christmas, and offered to show it to the little stranger. But she only turned away her head, and wouldn't look at it.

Grace, the youngest daughter, tried next; but she was puzzled to know what to do. Yet she was not willing to give up, but stood looking at the child and feeling great pity for her. At last she went and sat down by the side of the crying child, and *she cried too*. Presently she took the poor child's hand into hers and stroked and patted it gently. Then she said to her tenderly, "Don't cry, dear. No one will hurt you here. We only want to love you, and be good to you." Then she put her little arms round the stranger's neck, and took her head upon her shoulder, and gently kissed her.

The little girl stopped crying. She looked earnestly in the face of this new friend, and then dashing away her tears she said—"I'll go anywhere with *you*."

So Grace took the little one by the hand and led her into the parlour.

"Well, girls," said her mother, "Grace has found out the secret. The four letters to which I referred spell the word l-o-v-e. Love has greater power than anything else in the world."

And love is gentle. The power of love is the power of gentleness. We see in this story how great this power is. Let us take one more example of the power of gentleness.

A MOTHER'S VOICE.

A good lady, living in one of our large cities, was passing a drinking saloon one day, just as the keeper of it was turning a man into the street. He was quite young, but very pale. His haggard face and wild eyes showed that he had been drinking, and was far gone on the way to ruin. He was swearing dreadfully, and shaking his clenched fist at the man who had thrust him out of the saloon. He was so blinded with passion that he did not see the lady who stood near him, till she laid her hand on him and asked, in a gentle, loving voice—"What's the matter?"

The young man started as though a heavy blow had struck him. He turned quickly round, paler than before, and trembling from head to foot. He looked at the lady for a moment, and then said—

"Oh! I thought it was my mother's voice; it sounded so strangely like it! But *her* voice has long been hushed in death."

"You had a mother, then, who loved you?" said the lady.

He burst into tears as he said: "Oh yes, I had an aged mother, and she loved her boy. But since she died everything has gone against me. I am lost;—lost to everything that is good,—lost for ever."

"No, not lost for ever; for God is merciful and gracious, and His pitying love can reach the chief of sinners," said the lady in a low sweet voice, and her words seemed to have a wonderful effect upon the young man.

As the lady passed on her way the young man followed her. He noticed the number of the house she entered, and wrote down in his pocket-book the name that was on the door-plate. Then he went on his way with new thoughts and feelings stirred in his breast.

Years passed away, and the kind lady had forgotten all about this incident, when one day a stranger called at her house and sent up his card, asking permission to speak with her. Wondering who it could be, she went down to the parlour and found a noble-looking, well-dressed gentleman. He rose respectfully to meet her, and holding out his hand, said—

"Pardon me, madam, for this liberty; but I have come many miles to thank you for the great service you rendered me a few years ago," said he in a trembling voice.

"I am puzzled to know what you mean, sir," said the lady, "for I do not remember to have ever seen you before."

"I have changed so much," said the young man, "that I do not wonder you have forgotten me. But though I only saw you once, I should have known you anywhere. And your voice, too, is so much like my mother's."

The moment these last words were spoken the lady remembered the poor young man to whom she had spoken kindly in front of the drinking saloon, so long before. She saw him weeping, and she wept with him.

Presently the gentleman wiped away his tears, sat down, and told the lady that the few gentle words she spoke to him on that day had been the means of saving him from ruin, and of making him a useful man.

"Those words—'*Not lost for ever,*' followed me," said he, "wherever I went; and it always seemed to me like my mother's voice speaking to me from the grave. I repented of my sins, and resolved to live as Jesus and my mother would like to have me live, and I am thankful to say, that by the grace of God I have been able to resist temptation, and do some good in the world."

"I never dreamed there was so much power in a few kind words," said the lady.

But we know there *is*. There is great power in gentleness. Here we see the beauty of the King's lessons. And this is a good reason why we should learn and practise this lesson of gentleness.

But, in the second place there is—GREAT PLEASURE—*in gentleness.* And this gives us another view of the beauty of the King's lesson.

When you see a column of finely-polished marble you know how smooth it is, and how pleasant it is to draw your hand slowly over its glossy surface. Well, what the fine polish is to that marble, gentleness is to our words and actions. It takes the roughness from them and gives a smoothness which is very pleasant to those who are about us.

BEAUTY OF THE KING'S LESSONS.

When we go into the woods in summer time, we see the soft, downy moss that grows over the rocks; and when we tread on that moss, or sit on it, or lie down on it, we know how pleasant it is to have the sharp, rough corners of the rock all covered over by that beautiful moss! Well, just what that velvet moss is to the rock, a loving, gentle spirit is to our words and conduct. It covers up the sharp corners, and smooths down the rough places, and helps to make all that we do, and say, pleasant to those about us. And as gentleness is like moss, we ought to learn and practise this lesson, and then we shall have the moss of gentleness growing around us everywhere.

LENDING A PAIR OF LEGS.

Sometimes we ask our friends to "Lend us a hand," and sometimes we hear them say, "Lend me your eyes;" but here is a story of a boy who lent a pair of legs to another boy.

Some boys were playing at base-ball, in a quiet shady street. Among their number was a little fellow, about twelve years old, who was lame. He was pale, and feeble, supported on two crutches, and found it hard work to move about, even with the help that the crutches gave him.

The lame boy wanted very much to take part in the game. He did not see how much his lameness would be in his own way, and in the way of the other boys.

His companions good-naturedly tried to persuade him to stand aside, and let another take his place. They did not like to hurt his feelings, by telling him that his lameness would be in the way. Still he wanted to join. "Why, Jimmy," said one of them at last, "you know you can't run."

"Hush! hush!" said another of the boys, "I'll lend him my legs. When his turn comes, I'll run for him, and you can count it to him." So he took his place by Jimmy's side ready to lend him his legs, and run for him, when his turn came.

"You know," said this kind-hearted boy, aside to his companions, "if you were like him, you wouldn't want to be told of it, all the time."

That boy had learned the lesson of gentleness. And pleasant indeed it must have been to see him practising it. What lots of nice soft moss there would be, on all the rocks near his house.

PAWS AND CLAWS.

"Mother," said little Nanny, "sometimes pussy has paws, and sometimes she has claws; isn't that funny? She pats with her paws, and plays prettily; but she scratches with her claws, and then I don't love her. I wish she had no claws, but only soft little paws. Then she would never scratch, but would be always nice."

"Well, Nanny, dear," said her mother, "remember that you are very much like pussy. Those little hands, so soft and delicate, when well employed, are like pussy's paws, very pleasant to feel. But when they pinch, or scratch, or strike in anger, then they are like pussy's claws."

"Well, that's funny enough, mother. I never thought I was so much like pussy."

"You love pussy much," said her mother, "and you may learn a good lesson from her. When you think kind thoughts, and speak gentle, loving words, then you are like pussy with her nice, soft paws, and everybody will love you. But when you think bad thoughts, or give way to ugly tempers, and speak cross and angry words, then you are like pussy with her sharp, scratching claws, and no one can love you."

Nice, soft paws are much pleasanter, than sharp, tearing claws. And so gentleness is much pleasanter than anger or wrath, and this is a good reason why we should try to learn this lesson.

THE SAND-PAPER TONGUE

A gentleman who had learned well the lesson of kindness, one day heard a neighbour of his give a very rough answer to some boys who had asked him, in a polite way, how to find a particular street.

"Friend Jones," said the gentleman, "a man's tongue is either a piece of velvet or a piece of sand-paper; just as he likes to use it. I declare you use your tongue like a piece of sand-paper. Now, it's quite as cheap, my friend, to have a velvet tongue as a tongue of sand-paper, and a great deal pleasanter. Let's try the velvet tongue."

Think of the difference between a velvet tongue and a tongue of sand-paper. You know how soft velvet is, and how pleasant it is to handle it. And you know how rough sand-paper is, and how unpleasant it is to handle it. Sand-paper is stiff paper, which has fine sand or ground glass fastened on it with glue. It is used by cabinet-makers, who rub their furniture with it, so as to take off all the roughness. If you rub it on your hand, it will take the skin off, and make the blood come. Sand-paper, then, is very rough and disagreeable. And a sand-paper tongue is one that speaks rough, unkind words. These hurt our feelings just as the flesh is hurt when the sand-paper is rubbed over it. When we speak rough or angry words, we are using the sandpaper tongue, and making somebody's heart bleed

THE SOFT ANSWER.

A stout boy, who worked in a grocery store, was one day carrying a big basket filled with tea, coffee, sugar, oranges, and other good things, along a narrow lane, to a house at the end of the village. As he walked slowly along with his load, a merry little fellow came running in the opposite direction, singing like a lark on a sunny morning. He was a little careless, for he came plump against the grocer-boy's basket, and knocked it off his arm. Away rolled the bright golden oranges, and out went the parcels on the dusty path, very much

BEAUTY OF THE KING'S LESSONS.

to the vexation of the errand boy. With his face flushed, and his eyes flashing, he rolled up his sleeves, and squared off for a fight.

But the little fellow did not want to fight. He had no wish to injure the grocer's boy. So with a pleasant smile he said—

"I'm real sorry for what I've done. It was very careless in me. Indeed I didn't mean to upset your basket. I beg your pardon. Come, let me help you to pick up the things." These were soft words. There was a gentle spirit in them, and this melted the anger from the other boy's heart as the sunbeams melt the snow. They "turned away his wrath." He saw that nothing was to be gained by fighting, so he dropped his arm, and went to work to pick up the scattered goods. When everything was replaced the boys shook hands with each other, said "good morning," and went on their way, cheerful and happy.

Now suppose the boy who upset this basket, when he was spoken to crossly, had used hard words, instead of soft ones. What then? Why, there would have been a fight. Black eyes, and bleeding noses, and broken parcels, and squeezed oranges, and angry feelings, would have been the end of it. The lesson of gentleness practised prevented all this. Soft words are pleasant and blessed things. They are more precious than pearls. Let us remember this, and keep them ready to use whenever needed.

There is *great pleasure* in gentleness. Here we

see the beauty of this lesson of our King; and a good reason for learning it.

But, in the third place, there is—GREAT PROFIT—*in gentleness: and* here again we see the beauty of this lesson.

If people can only be sure of profit in anything they are asked to engage in, it has great weight with them. "Will it pay?" is a question often asked. And when there is a hope of good pay, men are ready to do almost anything.

But there is great profit in gentleness. It brings real, substantial benefits to those who practise it. Let us look at some examples of this.

THE POWER OF KINDNESS.

One day in winter, a heavily-laden team was going along one of the streets of Boston. It was just after a snow storm. Pretty soon the waggon got stalled in the snow, and the horses stopped. The kind-hearted driver, instead of getting angry at the horses, cursing them, and lashing them with his whip, got a shovel and cleared away the snow from before the wheels. Then he stepped up to the shaft horse, and patting him gently said in a kind voice: "Now, Billy, we are in a fix. You'll do the best you can, won't you?" The horse really seemed to understand what was said to him, and rubbed his head against his master's shoulder as if to say, "All right. I'll do my best." Then he started with a will, and carried the waggon straight through the snow.

A well-known gentleman who belonged to the Society for the Prevention of Cruelty to Animals was going by and saw what took place. He was so much pleased that, when he reached his office, he wrote a note at once to the owner of the team, and enclosed a ten-dollar bill, with the request that it should be given to "the driver who treated his horses so kindly."

Certainly that man found his gentleness profitable to him, not only in the ease and comfort with which he got out of the trouble with his horse, but also in the money that it brought him; and in what was worth much more to him, the respect which it secured to him from the gentleman who sent him the money.

KINDNESS NOT FORGOTTEN.

There was a boy who was born in England, but whose parents went to America while he was yet young. He was bound out as an apprentice near Newark, New Jersey, but is now a rich man. Not long ago he was riding with a friend. Pointing to a certain gateway, as they rode by, he said—

"When I was a boy on this place, I remember, one day, opening that gate to let a gentleman on horseback go out. He threw me a silver sixpence. It dropped in the dust and I could not find it. He saw that I had lost it and came back and kindly got off his horse and helped me to find it. As he handed it to me he spoke so gently and lovingly that I never could forget his kindness. Within the last few years I have had it in my power three times to save that gentleman from failing in business, and it gave me the greatest pleasure to do so, because of that sixpence which he gave me and the kindness with which he did it."

Now certainly that gentleman's kindness was very profitable to him. It kept him three times from failing in business. He never invested sixpence in all his life that yielded such good interest as the one he gave, so kindly, to that poor boy.

GENTLENESS AND ITS REWARD.

Two boys applied for a place in the store of a Boston merchant. One was older than the other, and had some experience in the business. He was a gentleman's son, and well-dressed. The other boy was the only son of a poor widow. His clothes were plain and threadbare, but clean and well-mended, and his face had a quiet, honest look, that was itself a good letter of recommendation. The elder lad, the gentleman's son, would no doubt have got the situation, if it had not been for a little incident that occurred at that time.

The two boys came together, at the hour appointed, to the gentleman's store. He happened to be on the door-step just as they came up. At that moment a poor shivering child crossed the street. As she stepped on

BEAUTY OF THE KING'S LESSONS.

the sidewalk, her foot slipped on the icy stones, and she fell in the half-melted snow.

The elder boy laughed rudely at her appearance, as he saw the water dripping from her ragged clothes; but the poor child cried bitterly as she searched for her lost pennies. Willie, the younger boy, hastened to her side and helped her. Two pennies were found in the snow; the others were, probably, in a little icy pool beside the curbstone. Willie rolled up his sleeve, and plunged his hand down into the water, groping about for the lost pennies. One was found. He handed this to the poor child, saying—

"I'm afraid, Sissy, that the other is lost."

"Then I can't get the bread," said the child, "and mammy and the children can have no supper."

"There's a penny," said Willie, taking one from a little purse which had very few in it, and then he washed his hand in the snow, and wiped it on his coarse white handkerchief. The other boy looked on with contempt, and said—

"You're a greenhorn, I guess."

But he was mistaken. The gentleman to whom they were both applying for the situation had seen and heard what had taken place. He made up his mind in a moment to give the situation to Willie, though he would, no doubt, have given it to the other boy, if it had not been for this incident. It proved to be an excellent situation for Willie, and I need scarcely say that he did well in it. Willie's gentleness gained him that situation. Certainly, he found it profitable.

Here is another very good story that illustrates this point very strikingly.

KINDNESS REWARDED.

Some time ago, a poor old widow woman lived on the line of the Baltimore and Ohio Railway, where it passes through a wild district of Western Virginia, in which are very few inhabitants. She had an only daughter. They lived in a log hut near a very deep gorge, which was crossed by the railway bridge. The widow and her daughter managed to support themselves by raising and selling poultry and eggs. In the summer season they gathered berries, and with other little articles, carried them to market. But it was a long and weary walk to the town where she sold these articles. The railway passed by her cabin to this town; but she could not afford to ride, and so trudged contentedly along on foot. The conductor of the train came to know this good old woman. He was a kind-hearted man. He had learned the lesson of gentleness, and loved to practise it whenever he had a chance; and so he often called to the old widow when she was in sight, and gave her a ride to or from the market town. This saved her many a weary mile. She felt very grateful to the conductor for his kindness, and the object of this story is to show how profitable his kindness proved to him.

One spring, in the stormy month of March, heavy rains had fallen. Roaring torrents of melting snow and ice came rushing down from the mountains into the gorge, near the old widow's hut. The flood arose in the darkness of the night, and she heard a terrible crash. The railway bridge was torn from its place, and its broken timbers dashed against the rocks below. It was almost midnight. The rain fell in torrents. It was dark as Egypt. The storm was howling terribly. In half an hour the express train would be due. What could be done to give warning of the awful danger threatening that train? It was terrible to think of the destruction that awaited it. But what *could she* do? She had hardly a whole candle in her hut; and no light she could make, of this kind, could burn in that wild storm. Not a moment was to be lost. Quick as thought she resolved what to do. She cut the cord of her only bedstead, and shouldered the bedding; the bed-posts, the side pieces and head pieces. Her daughter followed with their two wooden chairs. They climbed up the steep embankment, and piled all their household furniture in the middle of the railway track, a few rods in front of the awful gorge through which the wild flood was dashing. She kindled the fire; and the distant rumbling of the train was heard just as the dry broken furniture began to burn. The bright blaze leaped up, and threw its red, glaring light a long way upon the track. But the fire would not last long, and she had nothing more with which to keep it burning.

The thunder of the train grew louder. But it was still five miles distant. Will they see it in time? Will they put on the brakes soon enough? The thought almost makes her wild. What else can she do? She tears off her dress. She fastens it to the end of a pole, plunges it into the fire, and then runs along the track waving the blazing signal round her head. Her daughter seizes a piece of the blazing bedstead and follows her mother's example in waving it round. The next moment will decide the fate of a multitude of passengers. The ground trembles under the old widow's feet. The great red eye of the engine bursts upon her as it turns a sudden curve. The train is at full speed; but the engineer sees that there is something wrong. A shrill whistle echoes through the hills. Its cry is—"Down brakes! down brakes!" The brakemen spring to their posts, and bend on the wheels with the strength which desperation gives. The wheels move slower and slower, and the panting engine finally stops in front of the widow's fire. It still gave light enough to show the bridge gone, and the yawning abyss, where the train and its passengers would have plunged into death and destruction, too horrible to think of, had it not been for the good widow's signal fire.

The conductor, the engineer, the brakemen, and passengers came to see what was the matter. And when they saw the bridge gone, and the dreadful gulf into which they had so nearly plunged, we can imagine how they felt. They did not thank the widow first; but kneeling down by the side of the engine, in the dim light of the burnt-out pile, amidst the rain and wind and pelting storm, they first thanked God, who had made use of the widow woman to save them from such a terrible death. And then, with many tears, they

"The bright blaze leaped up, and threw its red glaring light a long way upon the track."

thanked her for what she had done. Then they made a collection for her on the spot. Afterwards the railway company, on hearing of her noble act, gave her money enough to make her comfortable for the rest of her life. This was right, and generous, and noble.

Surely that conductor was well paid for his kindness to the old widow woman. This story proves the great profit there is in gentleness.

"A soft answer turneth away wrath."

Thus we have seen that there is—*great power—great pleasure*—and *great profit* in gentleness. This shows us the beauty of this lesson of our King, and should lead us all to try and learn—the lesson of gentleness.

There was an old gentleman who was remarkable for his gentleness. When a young man he was known to have had a violent temper. He was asked how he managed to overcome his bad temper? His answer was a short but a wise one. Let us remember it in connection with this sermon. He said it was—" By praying to God, *and speaking low.*"

When persons are angry, they raise their voices and speak loud. To overcome anger and learn the lesson of gentleness, we must—"*pray to God and speak low.*"

IX.

THE BEAUTY OF THE KING'S TITLES.

"THE LORD IS MY ROCK."—2 *Samuel* xxii. 2.

IX.

THE BEAUTY OF THE KING'S TITLES.

JESUS COMPARED TO A ROCK.

If you and I go and stand by the cradle in which a baby is sleeping, no matter how much we love it, or feel interested in it, we cannot tell what sort of a person it will be when grown up. No one can tell this of any ordinary baby. But it was different with Jesus, when He lay, as an infant, in the manger at Bethlehem. If we had gone with the shepherds to worship Him, we might have taken our Bibles with us, and as we stood there, gazing in wonder at the infant Saviour, we might have opened our Bibles; and turning to one passage after another, that the prophets had written about Him, we might have told just what sort of a person He was going to be. It had been foretold about Him that He was to be a Prophet—a Priest—a King—a Shepherd—a Father—a Friend—a Counsellor—a Comforter—a Leader—a Refuge and a Shield. He was compared to a great many things that were useful, and interesting, and beautiful. And, among these He was compared to a Rock. David was speaking of Jesus, in the chapter in which our text is found, when he said—"The Lord is my Rock." And there are a great many other places, in which He is spoken of as a Rock. The prophet Isaiah says in one place—"In the Lord Jehovah is everlasting strength" (chap. xxvi. 4). In the Hebrew Bible the word for "everlasting strength" means also—"the Rock of Ages." We always think of Jesus when we sing that good old hymn,

> "Rock of Ages, cleft for me,
> Let me hide myself in Thee."

And it is right to think so. Here we see the beauty of Jesus our King in the titles applied to Him. Now, we are to think of Jesus as—*The Rock*.

And the question we have to try and answer is— What kind of a Rock do we find in Jesus?

There are four things about this Rock of which we must speak, if we wish to understand just what kind of a Rock it is that we find in Jesus.

In the first place, it is—A BROAD ROCK—*that we find in Jesus.*

Every other Rock is confined to some one particular place. If you want to get any benefit from it, you must go to the place where the rock is found.

We have all heard, for example, about the "Rock of Gibraltar." This is a great mountain of rock in the southern part of Spain, at the entrance into the Mediterranean Sea. It belongs to England. The English people have made a fort or citadel out of that mountain Rock. Rooms and galleries are cut through the heart of it. Port-holes for cannon are made through those walls of solid rock. That is the strongest fortress in the world. It is so strong that it cannot be taken. The heaviest cannon-balls can make no impression upon it. If you and I were in danger of being attacked, we should be entirely safe, provided we could only get into that rocky fortress of Gibraltar. But suppose that we are in danger here, in our own country, and that strong rock is thousands of miles away ; will it be of any use to us? No. It is too far off. We cannot reach it. But when we think of Jesus as our Rock, He is not, like the Rock of Gibraltar, confined to one particular place. He is in every place. He is indeed a *broad Rock*. This Rock is *so* broad that it may be found in every country. In any part of the world it is easy to get on this Rock. This is what David meant to teach us, when he said, "From the ends of the earth will I cry unto Thee— when my heart is overwhelmed—lead me to the Rock" (Psa. lxi. 2).

If we want to know how broad this Rock is, we must notice what sort of people get on it.

WHERE AM I GOING?

One fine summer evening, as the sun was going down, a man was seen trying to make his way through the lanes and cross-roads that led to his village home. His unsteady, staggering way of walking showed that he had been drinking, and though he had lived in that village more than thirty years, he was now so drunk that it was impossible for him to find his way home.

Quite unable to tell where he was, at last he uttered a

dreadful oath, and said to a person going by, " I've lost my way ; where am I going ?"

The man thus addressed was an earnest Christian. He knew the poor drunkard very well, and pitied him greatly. When he heard the inquiry—" Where am I going ?" in a quiet, sad, solemn way he answered,

" To ruin."

The poor staggering man stared at him wildly for a moment, and then murmured, with a groan—" *That's so.*"

" Come with me," said the other kindly, " and I'll take you home."

The next day came ; the effect of the liquor had passed away, but those two little words, tenderly and lovingly spoken to him, did not pass away. " To ruin ! To ruin !" he kept whispering to himself. It's true, I'm going to ruin. O God, help me, and save me."

Thus he was stopped in his way to ruin. By earnest prayer to God, he sought the grace which made him a true Christian. His feet were established on the Rock. It was a rock broad enough to reach that poor, miserable drunkard, and it lifted him up from his wretchedness, and made a useful, happy man of him.

THE INFIDEL CAPTAIN.

A minister of the Gospel was once travelling on one of our western steamboats. The captain of this boat was a very profane man, and was in the habit of swearing dreadfully against religion and the Bible. He took special pains to do this in the hearing of this good minister. The captain was a very violent man, and most persons were afraid of speaking to him about religion.

But this minister knew no fear. His heart was full of courage and of kindness. He believed that however wicked a man may be, there is always some good spot in his heart that, if it be touched wisely and kindly, may lead him to better things. So he took an opportunity one day of speaking to the captain on the subject of religion. This made him angry, and he spoke with great violence against the Scriptures, and the story of the life of Jesus. He said he believed the Bible was full of lies and nonsense.

When he got through, the minister simply said to him—" Captain, did you ever read the New Testament?"

This was an unexpected question. But the captain was honest.

"No," said he, "I can't say that I ever did."

"Will you promise me to read it through? And then when we meet again, we will have a talk about it."

This was said so kindly and pleasantly that the captain was obliged to say he would.

The minister gave him a Testament and then they separated.

Some weeks after this, that minister was going down the river again on the same boat. Here he met his friend, the captain. As soon as he looked at him he saw that a change had taken place in him.

You know when you look at a house by night, you can tell in a moment whether there is a light in it or not. If there be no light in it, the windows will look gloomy and dark. But if there be a light in it, you will see its beams shining brightly through the windows.

When we are not Christians we have no true light in our souls. But when we learn to know and love Jesus, He kindles the hope of heaven in our souls, and that lights them up, as if there was a sun shining within us. The minister shook the captain warmly by the hand, and said to him—

"Well, my friend, what do you think about the Testament now?"

"Sir," said the captain, "I thank you with all my heart for giving me that blessed book. I had not read far in it before I found that I was a great sinner. Then I was in great trouble. But I read on, and pretty soon I found that Jesus is a great Saviour; just what I needed. I began to pray to Him. On board this crowded boat, going up and down the river, I sought Him, and I found Him; or rather I ought to say that He found me. He pardoned my sins, and comforted me, and blessed me, and now I am as happy as the day is long, and I want everybody to know and love Jesus."

So the captain found this Rock in his journeys up and down the river. He got on the Rock, and it made him glad. What a broad Rock this is!

NO WAY TO CHRIST.

A minister of the Gospel was going out of his church one Sunday, after a very solemn service. Standing in the aisle he met a young man whose eyes were filled with tears, and who seemed to be in great distress. The young man came up to him and said, "Sir, can you tell me the way to Christ?"

"No, my friend," said the minister, "I cannot tell you the way to Christ."

"I beg your pardon," was the young man's answer, "but I thought you were a minister of the Gospel."

"So I am," he replied.

"And you cannot tell me the way to Christ?"

"No, I cannot tell you the way to Christ, because Christ Himself is the way; and there is no way *to* Him. You are thinking of Christ as up in heaven, or a long way off from you. This is not so. He is here. He is everywhere. He is nearer to you than I am now. He is ready to hear and waiting to bless you. Open your heart to Him. Tell Him what you want. Ask Him to pardon, and save, and bless you. Then believe His word when He promises to do so. And then, as surely as God lives, you will be saved." That young man did as he was told, and he soon found joy and peace in believing.

And if you and I should go round the world, we should find the same thing true everywhere. In Europe, in Asia, in Africa, in the islands of the sea, we might say to those who asked us the way to Jesus—"There is no way to Him, because He Himself is the way, and He is everywhere."

And so, when we speak of Jesus as "The Rock," we may well say that He is—a *broad* Rock.

But, in the second place, Jesus is—A HIGH ROCK—*as well as a broad one.*

David's prayer was—"Lead me to the *Rock* that is *higher than I.*" We think of heaven as a *high* place. And so it is. God calls it—"The *high* and holy place" (Isaiah lvii. 15). And one reason why we may speak of Jesus as higher than we are, is because He is in heaven, and we are on earth. But there is another sense in which we use this word "high." We apply it to *character*, as well as to *place*. For example, we sometimes say of a person in whom we have no confidence, that he is a mean, *low* fellow. Then we use the word *low* as meaning *bad*—a bad character. And so, on the other hand, when speaking of a person who is good, and honest, and noble-hearted, we say he has a *high* character. And so the word *high* sometimes means that which is noble or good. And Jesus may well be called *high* in this sense; because He is the best and noblest of all beings. And He not only has this character Himself, but He makes those who know and love Him share it with Him. It has been well said that—"A Christian is the *highest* style of man." And this is true of boys and girls too. And so we may well say that when we become Christians we are led to a "Rock that is *higher* than we are." It makes us better than we were before. Those who are really on this Rock may truly be said to be on a *high* Rock, because they are on a Rock that will help them to become good, and kind, and generous, and noble. Let us look at some examples of those who are on this high Rock, and see what kind of persons they are.

"*MY 'MANCIPATION BOOK.*"

In the year 1834, the British and Foreign Bible Society sent a large number of copies of the New Testament and Psalms to the West India Islands, to be distributed among the negroes there. The distribution of these books took place at the time of the Emancipation of the negroes, or their freedom from slavery. They came to think that, somehow or other, the Bible was the cause of their freedom; and so, they were accustomed to call it their "'Mancipation Book."

Some time after this, a Christian lady, who wished to make herself useful, was visiting one afternoon at a negro hut on one of the plantations. After talking, for awhile, with the negro woman who lived there, she saw a fine large copy of the Bible on the shelf, and pointing to it, she said—

"Nanny, what handsome book is that you have there?"

"O missis! dat's my 'Mancipation Book."

"But it's of no use to you, Nanny, because you can't read it."

"For true, missis, me no able to read him; but me pickaninnies (children) can."

"Well, but your pickaninnies have books of their own to read. You might spare that for somebody who can read, but who has no Bible."

"No, missis," replied Nanny, with great earnestness, "no; me no able to spare him at all. Dat book de one watchman for me house."

"How so?" asked the lady.

"Why, missis, beforetime, Nanny's temper used to rise too strong for her. Me no able to keep him down at all. But now, when de bad temper would rise, de book stan dar, and him say, 'No, no, Nanny, you no go for to do dat. Dat is wicked.'"

And so Nanny, who had been one of the most ill-tempered and disagreeable persons on the plantation, became, through the grace of God, a thoroughly changed woman. The mere sight of the Bible, which she could not read, was a help to her, in subduing her bad temper. It was a *high* Rock to which she was led, when she became a Christian. It was higher than she was, and gave her a better character than she could have had, if she had not been led to that Rock.

THE TOULOUSE GALLEY-SLAVE.

Many years ago, in some countries of Europe, when a person committed an offence against the laws, he was condemned to work, for a number of years, as what was called "a galley-slave." These galleys were large vessels, which were moved along, by a great number of heavy oars. The men who rowed these oars were chained to the seats on which they sat. The work they had to do was very severe, and the treatment they received was hard and cruel.

On one occasion, a young man, belonging to a good family, had fallen into bad company. He joined his companions one night in doing something very wrong. He was taken up, tried, and sentenced to serve for seven years, among the galley-slaves, in the harbour of Toulouse, in France. There, he had time to think over his evil ways. He was led to repentance, he prayed for pardon, and became a Christian. Even on board the galley-slave ship he was led to this high Rock. What a high character it gave him we shall see directly.

Not long after this, he contrived to make his escape from the slave ship. He disguised himself, and set off for his home in a distant part of the country. While pursuing his journey he stopped one night at a cottage by the roadside, and asked for a night's lodging. It was freely given to him. As he sat with the family, at their evening meal, he found they were in great distress. Their rent, amounting to forty francs, was due. They were unable to pay it, and father, mother, and six children, were to be turned out of doors in a few days. The young man was greatly distressed for them, and lay awake the rest of the night, thinking it all over. There was only one thing he could do to help them, and that he resolved to do.

In the morning he told the cottager that he was a slave who had just made his escape from one of the galleys in the harbour of Toulouse. "Now, I know," says he, "that a reward of fifty francs is always given to any one who brings back an escaped slave. I have no one depending on me for support. But you have a wife and six children. I will gladly go back and serve out my time in the slave ship rather than have you and your family turned out of home. I shall feel then that I am doing some good in the world. So just put a rope round me, and lead me back to the city. Then with the fifty francs you will receive, you can pay your rent and have ten francs left for your family."

"No," said the honest cottager, "I would starve with my family, rather than do anything so mean as that."

"Then I will go back and give myself up, and you will have to see your family suffer."

Finally, after much persuasion, he induced the man to do as he wished. The rope was tied round his body. The cottager led him back to the city, he delivered him up to the mayor. The fifty francs were paid over to him. But instead of going gladly away with his reward he stood sadly by. When he saw them fastening the chains on the noble young man he burst into tears. They asked him what this meant. Then he told of the young man's noble offer. This melted the hearts of all who heard it. The chains were taken off. He was set at liberty, honoured with many gifts, and sent to his home rejoicing. It was a high Rock on which that young man stood, and those who stand with him on it will share in his noble character. That Rock is Christ. He is a *high* Rock.

In the third place, this is—A SHELTERING ROCK.

Sometimes we find in a high rock, or on the side of a mountain, a place cleft out, nicely lined with soft moss. There you can sit down and find protection and comfort when the wind is blowing, or the rain is beating, or the storm is bursting. *That* is a sheltering rock. And it is such a rock as this that Jesus is compared to in the Bible. David is speaking of Him when he says:—" In the time of trouble He shall hide me in His pavilion, in the secret of His tabernacle shall He hide me; He shall set me up upon a rock" (Ps. xxvii. 5). Here is an illustration of the way in which the Lord fulfils this promise.

A city missionary one Saturday night was going home with a basket of provisions on his arm. Meeting a policeman, he asked him if any families had moved into that neighbourhood lately.

"Yes," he said, pointing to a building up an alley, "a poor woman and some children are living there now."

The missionary went to the house, rapped at the door and was admitted. The woman was sitting by a small light sewing. In the corner of the room were two little girls, from nine to twelve years old, playing.

"My good friend," said the missionary, "I am here to see, if you will let your girls attend Sunday-school to-morrow?"

"I would, sir, very gladly, if they had any suitable clothes to go in."

"The Lord will provide," said the missionary. "Have you no money?"

"Not yet, but I have committed my case into the Lord's hands."

"Have you anything to eat?"

"Nothing, sir."

"What will you do for breakfast?"

"Oh, sir; once I had a husband. He provided everything for me and my children. But now he is dead. Yet God my Maker is my husband, and He has promised to be a Father to the fatherless. We have committed all to Him, and have called on Him, in this our day of trouble. I am trusting in God to take care of a poor widow and her children in a strange place, and I know He will provide."

"Thank God for such faith," said the missionary, and handed her the basket, saying, "Here is the breakfast God has sent you, and before night you shall have clothing for your children."

"Oh, thank God for His faithfulness!" exclaimed the woman. "He hears and answers prayer. May He bless you!"

Here was a poor woman turning to this Rock in time of trouble, and finding shelter in it.

We need a shelter when we are in fear as well as when we are in trouble. And this is the view of this Sheltering Rock that Solomon gives us when he says, "The name of the Lord is a strong tower, the righteous fleeth into it and is safe" (Prov. xviii. 10). Here is a story to show how a little boy was sheltered when he was afraid.

This boy's name was Frank. He was about five

years old. He was very much afraid of rats and mice. On his way up to the room in which he slept at night he had to go through a large lumber room. When he saw the rats and mice run across this room it frightened him, and made him cling close to his mother's side.

One night, when bedtime came, Frank's mother was sick, and could not go with him. His father was reading the paper, and he told him to go up to bed by himself.

"O father," said he, "I'm afraid to."

"What are you afraid of?" asked his father.

"Afraid of the rats and mice in the big lumber room."

"Oh, very well, if that's all, I'll soon fix that."

Frank's father was an officer in the army, and was accustomed to give what is called a pass, or safe-conduct. This is a paper signed and sealed by the officer in command, and given to a person to carry with him. It requires those to whom it is shown not to hurt the person who bears it, but to let him pass on in safety. Frank had great faith in his father's passes, and indeed in any paper on which his father's name and seal were put.

So his father took a piece of paper and wrote on it, these words :—

"To all the rats and mice in the house, greeting :—

"You are hereby ordered to let my little boy Frank pass through the lumber-room, and all other rooms, at all times. This order will stand good till further notice is given. Any rat or mouse disobeying it will be punished according to law. Witness my hand and seal."

His father then signed his name to it, and sealed it with a big red seal, and gave it to his little boy. He thanked his father for it, and kissed him, and went up to bed without a single fear. When he came to the door of the lumber-room, he flung it wide open, and said, "Ho, you rats and mice, you can't hurt me, because I've got my father's pass!"

Frank's faith in his father's pass freed him from all fear. Now this was only a make-believe pass. But Jesus, our Sheltering Rock, gives us a real pass that should keep us from all fear. He promises to "give His angels charge over us to keep us in all our ways; and that no evil shall befall us, neither shall any plague come nigh our dwelling" (Ps. xci. 10, 11). This is a real pass. We may carry it with us wherever we go, and if we only have the same kind of simple, childlike faith in it that Frank had in his father's pass, it will keep us safe not only from all danger, but from all fear of danger. We shall feel that "The Lord is our Rock." And we shall know that He is *a Sheltering Rock.*

The last thing to speak of about this Rock is that it is—A WELL-FURNISHED ROCK.

Sometimes we see a great rock that has ferns growing on it. There is plenty of nice soft moss and beautiful flowers there, and streams of clear, cold, sparkling water are flowing down from it. And in the Bible we read of honey being found in some rocks, and oil also. And sometimes gold and silver, and diamonds and other precious gems, are found on rocks. And if we had a rock on which all these beautiful and valuable things could be found, it would be very proper to speak of that as a "well-furnished rock." But I suppose there is no one rock in all the world on which all these things could be found. But we have just such a Rock in our Blessed Saviour. He is indeed "a well-furnished Rock." Everything that we need for the happiness and salvation of our souls, both in this world and in the world to come, we find in Him. David is speaking of those who are on this Rock, when he says, "Those who seek the Lord *shall want no manner of thing that is good*" (Ps. xxxiv. 10). And the apostle is speaking of those who are on this Rock, too, when he says—"My God shall supply *all your need* from the riches of His grace in Christ Jesus" (Phil. iv. 19).

"I've been on this Rock for forty years," said an aged Christian, "and it grows brighter all the time." What a blessed thing to be on such a Rock.

A TOUCHING INCIDENT

A little Sunday-school girl, seven years old, was on this Rock. She was taken sick, and having no home of her own, was taken to an hospital to die. Night came on. Nothing was heard in the room where she was but the ticking of the great clock in the hall, as its pendulum swung backwards and forwards, saying — tick —tick—tick. Thus the hours were struck, as they rolled slowly away. The clock had just struck—one—

when the voice of the little sufferer was heard—clearly, but softly—repeating this verse of her Sunday-school hymns—

> "Jesus, the name to sinners dear,
> The name to sinners given;
> It scatters all their guilty fear,
> It turns their hell to heaven."

Then all was silent again. Nothing was heard but the sound of the great clock as it went on ticking.

Presently, that same sweet voice was heard again repeating another verse about Jesus, the well-furnished Rock on which she was resting:—

> "Happy, if with my latest breath
> I may but gasp His name;
> Preach Him to all, and cry in death
> Behold, behold the Lamb!"

The nurse hastened to the side of the little sufferer, but she was too late. The angels had come before her, and had taken the dear child's happy spirit, from the lower ledge of the Rock on which she had rested, to its glorious, sunny heights in heaven.

A PRAYER IN THE WOODS.

A poor crippled orphan boy was on this Rock. Hear what he says of the help that he found on it.

"In the summer of 1874 it was necessary for me to go to Lowell, a distance of thirty miles. I had no money, and knew not how to get there. I asked the station agent and conductor for a ticket. They said they were not allowed to give tickets away. Not knowing what to do, I left the depot and went into the woods, some distance from the station, where I could be alone. Then I kneeled down and told my trouble to that Friend who is able to provide, and who is rich unto all that call upon Him. I told Him all about my difficulty, and asked Him, either to give me the money, or provide some way by which I might get to Lowell. I rose from my knees feeling sure that the Lord had heard me, and that I should get help in some way. As I turned to go out of the woods I heard some one say, 'Halloo! there.'

"I looked round with surprise, not knowing that anybody was near me.

"'Halloo!' said the stranger, 'I never heard such a prayer as that. What made you pray so?'

"I told him I was in want, and trouble, and had no one to tell it to but my Saviour.

"'You want money, don't you?' he said. 'The Lord has sent it to you; here is five dollars. It's always best to go and tell the Lord when you are in trouble. He knows how to help. Now go and use the money.'

"I thanked the stranger, and I thanked the Lord, who is no stranger to me, and then I went on my way, feeling very happy, and thinking about that sweet promise—'*My God shall supply all your need.*'"

And so we see how truly this may be called "a well-furnished Rock."

Here is one more illustration to show us how surely we may expect to find everything we need, whether it be little or great, on this Rock.

MASSA JESUS SEE 'EM.

A poor old woman, in one of the West Indian islands, was once in great poverty. Times were hard; she was feeble and unable to work. What distressed her most was, her shoes were so bad that she could not go to church without getting her feet wet, which always made her ill. She was a good Christian woman, who had long been on this blessed Rock, and had found out, by happy experience, what a well-furnished Rock it is. Sunday was coming again, and as the weather was wet it made her sad to think that there was no prospect of her getting to church.

But she said to herself—"My blessed Master say, 'Ask, and ye shall receive.' So me ask Him to help me now. Den me take de ole shoes, and kneel down, and say—'O Massa Jesus, look at dese ole shoes. Please do. Dey all broke. Me no able go to church any more in dem; do, Massa, help me.'

"Den me put 'em down, and feel quite cheery like. Me know Massa Jesus see 'em; dat enuf. In de evening some one come to de door and knock; rap—rap—rap. 'Who's dar?' me say. 'It's me, mammy,' says Mr. D.'s little boy. 'Massa sent dis parcel for you.' When de boy gone me open de parcel, and dar me find a pair of new shoes! Me know dat Massa Jesus sent 'em, and me heart too much glad. Oh, how me praise Him!" And so we see how truly this may be called a well-furnished Rock, because everything that we need for our bodies, or for our souls, may be found on it.

It is a *broad* Rock—a *high* Rock—a *sheltering* Rock—and a *well-furnished* Rock. How thankful we should be that there *is* such a Rock! If God has brought us on this Rock, by teaching us to know and love Jesus, we should be very cheerful and happy. And we should do all we can to let other persons know about this Rock, and try to get them on the Rock. This is one of our King's titles; and we see the beauty of the King in His titles.

"The Lord is my Rock."

X.

THE BEAUTY OF THE KING'S TITLES.

"I AM THE BREAD OF LIFE."—*John* vi. 35.

X.

THE BEAUTY OF THE KING'S TITLES.

JESUS THE BREAD OF LIFE.

THESE are words that Jesus spake in reference to Himself. And here we have another of the beautiful titles by which we learn to know Him. This title is not so striking as some of the others given to Him in the Bible. It is very plain, and practical, but very instructive.

We know a good deal about bread. It is on our tables all the time. We see it, and handle it, and eat it, every day. And we should be very thankful that Jesus has been pleased to compare Himself, not only with suns and stars, which are very far off, but also with things that are as familiar to us as our daily bread. "I am the bread of life." Our lesson from this text is—*Jesus compared to bread.* There are three reasons for this comparison; and in each of them we see what beauty there is in this title of Jesus our King.

Jesus may be compared to bread, in the first place, because bread is—A NECESSARY THING.

Bread is the most necessary of all things. But perhaps some of you may be ready to say, "No, that cannot be; because, if we had no bread, we could still live on other articles of food."

This is so. But then you must remember that when Jesus uses the word bread here, He does not mean by it that one article of food which we call bread—the substance which we make out of flour, by kneading it, and baking it. He uses the word bread here, to denote *food* of any kind. He was speaking to the Jews about the manna which God sent to their fathers when they were in the wilderness. That manna was their bread—their food. It was the only thing they had to eat as they journeyed through that desert land.

Suppose we could get nothing else to eat but bread. Then bread would be absolutely necessary for us. If we were without it we must die. And Jesus is compared to bread for this reason. It is necessary for us to have Jesus—to know Him, and love Him—if we wish our souls to live. There is nothing else, in the world, that can make the soul alive, and keep it alive, but the knowledge of Jesus, or what we learn about Him in the Bible.

If a person is hungry, and starving for want of food, then nothing is more necessary for that person than bread. But until we know Jesus our souls are hungry and starving. He alone can feed them. And He may well be compared to bread. because this is so necessary for us.

THE BEAUTY OF THE KING'S TITLES.

THE WORM IN A CIRCLE OF FIRE.

There was an Indian once who had become a Christian. He was so full of thankfulness to Jesus for pardoning his sins, and saving his soul, that he was never tired of talking about Him, and of telling his friends what a wonderful Saviour He was.

One day, a friend asked him what it was that Jesus had done for him, that led him to be always talking so much about Him? Instead of replying in words, the grateful man took *this* way of showing what Jesus had done for him, and how necessary he had found His help to be.

He took some dry chips, and little bits of wood. With these he made a circle about a foot in diameter. In the midst of this circle he placed a worm. Then he set fire to the circle of dry materials, and instantly there was a wall of fire blazing all round the poor worm. The worm crawled up to the edge of the fire, first on one side, and then on another. And at last, finding there was no way of escape for it anywhere, it went to the middle of the circle, as far from the fire as it could get, and then lifted its head up towards the sky, as much as to say that there was no help for it, unless it should come from above. Then the Indian put his finger down and let the worm crawl up on it, and so lifted it out from the danger that surrounded it.

"There," said the Indian, "you see what Jesus did for me. God was angry with me for my sins. His anger surrounded me on every side, just like that circle of fire. I had looked everywhere for help, but could not find it. Then Jesus reached forth His hand and saved me. Do you wonder that I love to tell about what He has done for me?"

THE NECESSITY OF A DOOR.

Johnnie was a little fellow only four years old. One Sunday morning it rained, and was too wet for Johnnie to go to church, so his father and mother went and left their little boy at home in charge of a servant-boy named Sammy. He was a good, faithful boy, and was trying to serve Jesus. All Johnnie's playthings were put away except the pussy cat. So Johnnie played awhile with kitty, and they got along very well together till he undertook to lift kitty up by her ears, as he had seen Sammy do with his rabbits. Kitty didn't like this at all, so she cried—meow—and gave Johnnie a scratch on the back of his hand. He dropped kitty very quickly She jumped out of the window and got away from him.

"Oh, dear," said Johnnie. "I wish I was in church."

"Suppose we play church?" said Sammy.

"Very well," said Johnnie, "you be the minister, and preach, and I'll be the congregation, and listen."

So Sammy took the big Bible and looked over it awhile, and then said—

"Now, Johnnie, here's a nice little text with only four words in it, and as you are a little boy, four years old, there'll be a word for each year of your life. This is the text,

"'I am the door.' You see the first word is I. It has only one letter in it. This 'I' means the Lord Jesus, the good Saviour who loves little children.

"The second word is—'*am.*' This has two letters in it. When Jesus says '*I am* the door,' of course He doesn't mean that he really is a door like that through which we come into this room; but only that He is *like* a door.

"The third word is—'*the.*' This has three letters in it. Jesus says—'I am *the* door,' because He is the one only door by which we can enter into heaven.

"The fourth word is—'*door.*' This has four letters in it. A door lets us into the house. If there were no door we could not get in. So the Lord Jesus lets us into heaven. If it were not for Him we could not get in at all. A door keeps out the rain, and the dogs, and the thieves; so Jesus keeps away all dangerous and hurtful things out of His beautiful heaven. If we want to get into a house we must go straight to the door, and if we want to get to heaven, we must go to Jesus, and ask Him to let us in."

Then Sammy knelt down, and little Johnnie by his side, and they prayed that the dear Lord Jesus would help them to love and serve Him, and bring them to His beautiful home when they died.

THE INFIDEL AND THE TEXT.

One Sunday evening a young man who was an infidel was going to some place of pleasure. On his way a person spoke politely to him and handed him a tract. He took it, and in passing by a gas lamp, he paused to look at it for a moment, and read these words—"Though your sins be as scarlet, they shall be as white as snow."

"Pshaw! nonsense!" he cried; and then tearing the tract to pieces, he threw them away.

But though he threw the paper away, he could not throw away the words he had read on that paper. As he lay down to sleep that night—"Though your sins be as scarlet, they shall be as white as snow," seemed to be repeated in his hearing. "Nonsense," said he, "these words are not for me. I'm an infidel. I don't believe in such things." He went to sleep. In the morning he woke, but hardly had he opened his eyes, before these words came to him again: "Though your sins be as scarlet, they shall be as white as snow." Wherever he went they seemed to follow him. Morning, noon, and night, they were sounding in his ears. He tried to shelter himself in his infidelity; but he could not get these strange words out of his mind. At last he began to see that he *was* a sinner. He felt that he was a *great* sinner. He saw that his sins were as scarlet, but he could not tell how they were to be made "white as snow." The thought of his scarlet sins made him very unhappy; and he felt that he never could be happy again until these sins were forgiven. After remaining in this state for some time he went to church one Sunday evening, and heard the minister preach from the words—"The blood of Jesus Christ His Son cleanseth us from all sin." And as the minister went on to tell of that fountain which Jesus opened for sin and uncleanness when He died upon the cross, he learned that it is through faith in Him that scarlet sins can be made white as snow. And then he was happy in believing in Jesus.

All these illustrations show us how impossible it is to find pardon, happiness, or salvation, in any other way than through Jesus. They show how necessary Jesus is to us. And this is the first reason why Jesus may be compared to bread—because bread is *a necessary thing*.

The second reason why Jesus may be compared to bread is, that bread is A STRENGTHENING THING.

When we have no bread or food for our bodies, the flesh wastes away from our bones, and we have no strength left to enable us to work, or walk, or even to stand. Sometimes we hear of a vessel out at sea that has run short of provisions. All the men have been on short allowance of food for many days. Perhaps half a biscuit is all that each man has had to eat for twenty-four hours. After awhile, a strange vessel comes in sight. When it comes nearer, the suffering crew make signals of distress. The stranger lays to, that is, stops sailing. He sends a boat to see what is the matter. When the officer in charge of the boat reaches the deck of the vessel in distress, he looks round in surprise. He says to himself—"Is it possible that these are men? They look more like ghosts, or walking skeletons. How thin and hollow their cheeks! How wasted and shrivelled their limbs! How they totter when they try to walk! How weak they are! Hardly one of them has strength enough to hold the helm, or pull a rope, or furl a sail."

This is the effect produced upon the body by want of food. But when we have plenty of good bread, or wholesome food, it is very different. Then our cheeks are round, and full, and rosy. Our limbs are plump and strong. We can walk, or run, or work, with pleasure. We are ready for anything we have to do.

And it is just so with our souls. Jesus is the bread which they must eat. When we know Him, and believe on Him, and love Him, then we are living on Him. He becomes the bread of life to us. And as we eat this bread we find it to be a strengthening thing. It helps us to do our duty, and to find pleasure in doing it.

Now let us look at some illustrations of the strength which people get from knowing Jesus, and feeding on Him as the bread of life to their souls.

A LITTLE CHILD MADE STRONG.

"Not long ago," said a minister who was making a temperance speech—"a little boy in my Sunday-school, only six years old, was sent by his mother to fetch his father home from the tavern where he was in the habit of spending his evenings and his money. He found his father drinking with some other men. One of them asked the little fellow to take some beer. In a moment the boy firmly said—'No, I can't do that, for I belong to the Band of Hope.' 'Well, if you won't take the beer,' said the man, 'here's a penny for you to buy bull's eyes.' These are a kind of sugar plums with liquor in them. The boy took the penny and said—'I thank you, but I don't want the bull's eyes; I would rather put the money in the penny bank.'

"The men looked at each other for a few moments, and were silent. Then one of them said, 'Well, boys, I think this is a good lesson for us. The sooner we sign the pledge and put our pennies in the saving bank the better.' The men left the house at once, and several of them, at least, followed that boy's example."

Now this little boy was accustomed to pray to Jesus every day to help him to do right. He was eating the bread of life, and it was this which strengthened him to speak and act as he did on this occasion. The two little speeches that he made in that tavern were good temperance speeches, and they were very useful.

THE SAILOR'S RELIGION.

At a meeting for prayer held in a mission house in London, one Sunday evening, a sailor rose to say a few words.

"My friends," said he, "I want to tell you what religion has done for me. It has made me love my mother, from whom I ran away when a boy; and it has made me provide for my wife and children, whom I had long neglected and treated unkindly."

Here you see how weak and sinful this man was before he had learned to love Jesus; but when he knew

Him, and had eaten of the bread of life, it gave him strength to do what was right.

LEARNING TO OBEY.

When we are asked to do what we wish to do, it is very easy to obey. But if we wish, very much, to do one thing, and are told to do the very opposite thing, then it is very hard to obey. And we need the strength which comes from eating the bread of life to help us then.

In the village where a little girl named Susie lived, there was going to be a picnic. She wanted very much to go to it. Her mother knew how anxious Susie was to go. She was very sorry not to let her go, but there were good reasons why it was necessary for Susie to stay at home.

"Mother, can I go to the picnic this afternoon?" she asked after breakfast.

"No, Susie, my dear, I'm sorry to disappoint you; but you can't go."

Her mother expected to see her look disappointed, and begin to fret and worry. But instead of this she looked very pleasant, and went out of the room singing merrily. When she came back, by and by, her mother said—

"Susie, my child, I am glad you take the disappointment so pleasantly. I was afraid you would be very much put out, when you found that you couldn't go to the picnic."

THE BEAUTY OF THE KING'S TITLES.   221

"O mother! I have been praying to Jesus lately to put the 'Thy-will-be-done spirit' in my heart. I think He has heard my prayer, and it helps me very much."

This "Thy-will-be-done spirit" is a blessed spirit to have in our hearts. It will make it easy for us to obey. In trying to get this spirit, Susie was making use of Jesus as the bread of life to her soul. And she found that this bread was a strengthening thing.

A YOUNG HERO.

Not long ago, you remember, that the yellow fever prevailed in different parts of our southern country. Among other places the city of Memphis suffered greatly from this dreadful disease. In this city there was one family consisting of six persons—a father and mother, two sisters and two brothers. The fever entered their house. All the family were stricken down by it except the youngest of the boys, a little fellow about twelve years old. He was a Sunday-school scholar—a thoughtful, serious boy, who was trying to love and serve Jesus. There was no one but him to wait upon the rest of the family. He did the best he could, and acted like a little hero. He woke one morning to find his mother and one of his sisters dead. This almost broke his heart. While he was weeping by the bedside of his mother, the doctor came in. He tried to comfort the little fellow for awhile, and then said to him—

"Now, Charley, my boy, you must play the man for

the sake of the rest of the family, who are so very sick. You must dry up your tears, and wash away the marks of them from your face, and go in and wait upon the sick ones. You must try and look cheerful; and not let them know that your mother and sister are dead till they get better. It might kill them to know it now."

Poor Charley! this was a hard thing for him to do. But, like a brave little fellow as he was, he resolved to try. Lifting up his heart to Jesus, in a silent prayer for help, he went in, looking bright and cheerful.

When he was asked how his mother was, he said, "I think she is better now." He meant to say she was in a better world, though he did not like to say that. He helped to nurse them, till they all got well again, and he was not taken sick himself. But it was the help that Jesus gave him—it was eating the bread of life that strengthened him to do his duty so nobly.

CHEER HIM.

There was a fire once in a large city. While the upper stories of a handsome dwelling were wrapped in smoke, and the fire was raging fiercely in the lower stories, a loud shriek told the firemen that there was still some one, in the building, in danger of being burned to death.

In a moment a ladder was reared. The upper end of it had hardly touched the heated walls, before a brave young fireman sprang to the ladder, and rushed up the rounds of it on his errand of mercy. But stifled by the smoke, he stopped, and seemed as if he was on the point of going back, without entering the burning building.

The crowd of people looking on, watched him with intense interest; for they feared that a moment's delay might cost a precious life. That moment's pause seemed very long.

As they were almost trembling with fear, a voice from the crowd cried out—"Cheer him! cheer him!" In a moment a loud, ringing, wild "hurrah" burst from that excited multitude. The fireman heard the cheer. He started up amidst smoke and flame, and disappeared through one of the windows. And now that vast crowd is still as the grave. Every voice is hushed; and every eye is fixed on that window. How long the seconds seem! Will he come? is the question that every heart is whispering. And now look at the window. There is the blackened form of the fireman, and clasped in his arms he has a little child. It is saved from a dreadful death by the courage of that brave fireman. Noble fellow! How loudly the crowd cheer him as he comes down the ladder! and how well he deserves it! When he paused on his way up the ladder, he needed just a little more strength and a little more courage. And what he needed, that hearty cheer of the crowd gave him. And what that cheer did for the fireman, Jesus does for His people. He is the bread of life to them, and gives them all the strength and courage they need.

And so the second reason why Jesus may be compared to bread is, that bread is a strengthening thing.

But there is a third reason for comparing Jesus to bread, and this is—that bread is a SATISFYING THING.

When we are hungry, the desire for food is very strong. There is a sort of gnawing feeling in the stomach that makes us very uncomfortable. But when we get as much good bread as we want, and eat it, then that gnawing, craving feeling disappears. The wants of the body are supplied, and we feel satisfied.

And it is just the same with our souls. The soul can be hungry as well as the body. And when this is the case a great longing will be felt, which will make us unhappy. And what our souls need then is Jesus. He is the only bread that is suited to our wants. And when we learn to know Jesus, and believe in Him, then we really eat the bread of life, and our souls feel satisfied and happy.

JESUS A COMFORT.

A Christian lady was visiting an hospital full of sick and suffering people. Lying on one of the beds was a poor young German girl, whose name was Mena. She had been there five months. She was an orphan girl, and was suffering from a disease which never could be cured. The lady sat down by her bedside and said to her—" Mena, do you know the Lord Jesus?"

A sweet smile lighted up her face, and a look of joy passed over it, as she said, " Jesus, yes, I know Him.

THE BEAUTY OF THE KING'S TITLES.

I love Him. I tell Him all my troubles, and He comforts me. What could I do here all alone without Him?"

The lady opened her Testament and read part of the fourteenth chapter of John, beginning with the precious words—" Let not your heart be troubled, ye believe in God; believe also in me." When she had finished, the poor child said—

" Will you please find that for me in my Testament, and mark the place, so that I can read it for myself when you have gone away?"

The lady found it gladly, and read again about the "many mansions" that Jesus is preparing for those that love Him. Then she offered a short and simple prayer that the blessed Saviour would be near His suffering child, and bring her at last to the heavenly mansions. When she rose from her knees she saw tears of joy coursing down the cheeks of the poor young sufferer.

"Oh! come again; come again," she said; "it is so sweet to hear about Jesus!"

That dear child had learned to feed on Jesus as the bread of life, and she found it a satisfying and comforting thing, although she was sick in an hospital, and expected to stay there till she died.

THE QUEEN AND THE CHILD.

Frederick the Great, king of Prussia, had a palace at Schönhausen. One day Queen Elizabeth, the wife of

Frederick, was walking in the garden connected with this palace. Her gardener had a little niece, named Gretchen, with him in the garden. She was on a visit to her uncle. Gretchen lived in the city of Berlin. Her father was a gardener too. He was a poor man, but he was a Christian, and he had taught his little daughter to know and love Jesus. The queen talked with little Gretchen, and was so much pleased with her simplicity, and bright, intelligent answers to the questions she asked, that she told her uncle to let her come to the palace the next day, and make a visit.

So Gretchen dressed herself very neatly and went to the palace at the time appointed.

One of the court ladies who knew about it saw her coming, and told the queen, who was then at dinner. The good queen was much pleased to hear that her little visitor had come. She ordered her to be brought in at once. Gretchen ran up to her kind friend, courtesied to her very respectfully, and kissed her dress. At the request of the queen she was placed on a chair by her side, where she could see at once all the splendid sight which that table presented. There was a large company dining with the queen. Lords and princes, and officers of the army, and ladies were there, sparkling with gold and jewels. It was the first time this innocent child had ever seen such a sight, and the queen felt curious to know what effect it would have upon her.

Gretchen looked quietly at the costly dresses of the company, and at the beautiful dishes of china and gold that covered the table, and was silent for awhile Then while all the persons at the table were looking at her, she clasped her little hands, and closed her eyes, and repeated in a simple, touching way, this verse of a hymn her father had taught her:—

> "Jesus, Thy blood and righteousness
> *My* beauty are—my glorious dress;
> Midst flaming worlds in these arrayed,
> With joy shall I lift up my head."

The company were greatly surprised, and deeply moved. One of the ladies said to the queen, with tears in her eyes, "Happy child! We thought she would envy us, but we have much more reason to envy her."

That little girl knew Jesus as the bread of life, and she was so satisfied with this bread that she did not want the rich and beautiful things that were before her in that great palace.

I have one more story to illustrate this last point of our subject. It relates to an incident that took place, some years ago, in the city of Philadelphia. This story was told me by our dear friend, Mr. Charles E. Lex, who is now in heaven.

One day we were walking together up Chestnut Street above Nineteenth. As we passed by Dr. Rush's house, which you know stands there, Mr. Lex pointed to it and said, "I want to tell you a story, which you may perhaps find occasion some day to use in one of your sermons for the young.

"It is about—

"DR. RUSH AND THE POOR WOMAN.

"That house which Dr. Rush built was one of the largest and finest in the city. When it was finished the doctor furnished it with great care. The carpets, mirrors, and furniture were all made on purpose for it, and were of the most elegant and costly style. And besides these the doctor had a great many beautiful pictures, and pieces of very valuable statuary. He invited many of his friends to come and see his splendid house, and it was thought to be a great privilege to do so.

"One day when Dr Rush was coming out of his house, before he had moved into it to live there, he met an elderly woman named Mary, going by, whom he knew very well, as she sometimes did house-cleaning and other work for him. Mary was a poor widow woman who lived very plainly, by herself, in two small rooms. She was a member of the Church of the Epiphany—a good, earnest Christian woman, whose religion made her contented and happy.

"The doctor had known her for a long time, and he respected her very much, for her consistent, humble piety. As he met her in front of his splendid dwelling, he thought he would like to show her through it, and see what effect the sight of a house, so much larger and grander than she was accustomed to, would have upon her. So he invited her to come in, and see the new house. Mary went in with him. The doctor took her

THE BEAUTY OF THE KING'S TITLES.

through the house, and showed her all the beautiful things he had there. She looked at them very quietly; but did not seem to be as much impressed by what she saw as the doctor thought she would be. When they got through he said to her—

"'Well, Mary, what do you think of the house?'

"'It's very fine, sir, indeed; and I'm ever so much obliged to you for letting me see it. But it doesn't begin to compare with the house that I'm going to move into before long. Let me read you a little about this house.'

"Then she took a little Testament from her pocket, and turning to the last chapter of the Book of the Revelation, she read some of those beautiful verses, which describe the heavenly city that is to be the home of those who love Jesus; and ended by saying—'I hope, sir, you may have much enjoyment in your new house; yet you can't expect to live here very long. But Jesus says, of those who enter the house He is preparing for them, that—"they *shall go no more out.*" *I shall dwell in that heavenly home—for ever.*'"

How sweet this was! That good woman knew Jesus as "the bread of life," and she found this bread a satisfying thing.

Bread is a necessary thing—a strengthening thing—a satisfying thing. Here we have three good reasons why Jesus may be called "the bread of life." Let our earnest prayer be—

"LORD, EVERMORE GIVE US THIS BREAD!"

INDEX.

Affliction, rejoicing in, 87, 88.
Afraid, sin makes us, 139, 140.
African chief and the resurrection, 130-132.
Albert, Prince, the happy death of, 91.
Ambassador, the anxious, 151.
Angels, examples of their power, 55, 56.
   ,, Christ's kingdom rules the, 56.
Answer, a soft, like a lightning rod, 163, 164.
A young hero, 221.

Baby, come forth, 135.
Bills, paying, by prayer, 106, 107.
Blind boy's trust in his father, 148.
Book, my 'mancipation, 195.
Bread, Jesus compared to, 211.
   ,, a strengthening thing, 217.
   ,, a satisfying thing, 224.

Cheer him, 222.
Child, a little, made strong, 218.
Christ, no way to, 193.
   ,, titles given to, before His birth, 187, 188.
Church, the Scripture figures of the, 71.
Claws and paws, 172.
Comfort in God's presence, 145.
Cripple, the robber, 43.
Crown, the heavenly, 84.

INDEX.

Death, happy in, 46.
Door, a sermon on the, 214.
Dream, helped through a, 110–113.
Dying, illustration of, two boys diving, 133, 134

Examination, the final, 127.

Faith, a child's, 158, 159.
  ,, a boy's, 144.
Family, the King's Beauty of, 71.
   ,,   ,, large, 72.
   ,,   ,, illustrations of its size, 73–76.
   ,,   ,, how made one, 77.
   ,,   ,, wealthy, 78.
   ,,   ,, honourable in spirit, or let me wear two, 85, 86.
   ,,   ,, happy, 86.
Father, the orphan's, 78.

Galley-slave, the Toulouse, 196–198.
Gentleness, great power in, 164.
  ,, great pleasure in, 170.
  ,, great profit in, 176.
  ,, and its reward, 178–180.
Girl, the happy blind, 88–90.
Gipsy, the, fortune-teller, 129–130.

Heaven only told of in the Bible, 5.
  ,, Bible comparisons of, 5–8.
  ,, its beauty as a place, 7.
  ,, the perfection of beauty, 9.
  ,, the outside of, beautiful, 9.
  ,, the land beyond the mountains, 10.
  ,, its company, the beauty of, 11.
  ,, angels, the company of, 11, 12.
  ,, our relations, the company of, 12, 13.
  ,, children in : will they remain such? 13–15.
  ,, none strangers in, 15–17.

INDEX.

Heaven, the person and presence of Jesus in, 18–23
    ,,   preparation necessary for it, as seen in the story of the crane, 22, 23.
Helped through a dream, 110–113.
Hero, a young, 221.
Honour, the highest, 82.

Incident, a touching, 203.
Infidel, the, and the text, 215–217.

Jesus, the appearance of, on earth, 3.
    ,,   His glory and beauty in Heaven, 4, 5.
    ,,   person and presence of, what good men say of it, 18–20.
    ,,   person and presence of, what the Bible says of it, 20.
    ,,   the beauty of, the world full of illustrations of, 21.
    ,,   foretold as a King, 28.
    ,,   the beauty of, as a King, in that He makes His people good, 28–30.
    ,,   the beauty of, as a King, He makes His people peaceful, 35.
    ,,   as a King, makes happy, 42.
    ,,   a comfort, 224.

Kindness rewarded, 180–183.
    ,,   not forgotten, 177.
    ,,   the power of, 176.
Kind words, the power of, 100–102.
Kingdom, Christ's, the beauty of, 51, 52.
    ,,   Christ's, rules all the greatest things, 52.
    ,,   Christ's, rules the world, 53.
    ,,   Christ's, rules all the smallest things, 57, 58.
    ,,   Christ's, comforting by small things, 62–64.
    ,,   Christ's, ruling at all times, and in all places, 65–68.

Land, the, beyond the mountains, 10.
Lazarus, the raising of, showing the King's power, 108

Legs, lending a pair of, 171, 172.
Lightning-rod, a soft answer like, 163, 164.
Love, the power of, secret of four letters, 166, 167.

Massa Jesus see 'em, 206.
Mattie, how, learned to serve God, 30.
Million, a, how long to count, 53, 54.
Missionary, a city, and a basket of provisions, 199.
Moffatt, Rev. R., and the resurrection, 130–132.
Moss like gentleness, 171.

Necessary thing, a, 211.
Neighbours, the, and the hens, 40.

Obey, learning to, 220.
Old Jim Drayton, how, was made good, 33.

Paws and claws, 172.
Peace, the, that Jesus makes as King, 36.
  ,, how Jesus makes—Freddie's prayer, 36.
  ,,   ,,   beating Satan, 38.
Penitent boy thief, the, 30.
Pity, the, of Christ, how it draws to Him, 98.
Power, God's preserving, 113, 114.
  ,, a ground for trust, 146.
  ,, the King's, in raising Lazarus, 108.
  ,, in the engine of an ocean steamer, 109, 110.
Portrait, the eyes of a, keeping a girl from stealing, 141.
Prayer, a, in the woods, 204.
  ,, life saved by, 103–105.
  ,, getting out of trouble by, 105,
  ,, paying bills by, 106, 107.
  ,, of Jesus in His work, 101, 102.
Presence, the thought of God's, should lead to trust, 141.
  ,, comfort in God's, 145.
  ,, God's, a comfort in banishment, 142.
Profit, great, in gentleness, 176.
Promise, a, trust in, 155–157.

INDEX.

Promises, God's trust taught by, 153.
,, a child's trust in God's, 154.
,, faith in, 155.

Queen, the, and the child, 225-227.

Rats and mice, a pass to, 201,
Religion, a sailor's, 219.
Resurrection, the, how Jesus is, 117, 118
,, thoughts and lessons of, 119,
,, certainty of, 119.
,, proofs of certainty outside the Bible, 119.
,, day and night show its certainty, 119.
,, the seasons show its certainty, 120.
,, insects and frogs show its certainty, 120, 121.
,, its certainty from the Bible, 122.
,, illustrated by a sprouting walking-stick, 123.
,, very wonderful, 122, 123.
,, illustrated by skeleton coming to life, 123, 124.
,, the, in a moment, 125.
,, the beauty of, 125, 126.
,, the beauty of, seen in the transfiguration, 126.
,, its lesson, how to live, 127.
,, effect of hearing of, on African chief, 130-132.
,, and its lessons, how to die, 132-135.
Riches, the heavenly, 79.
Rock, Jesus a broad, 187, 188.
,, the broad, a drunkard on, 189, 190.
,, ,, the infidel on, 190-192.
,, Jesus a high, 194.
,, ,, a sheltering, 198.
,, ,, a well-furnished, 202.
Rush, Dr., and the poor woman, 228.

Sand-paper, the, tongue, 173.
Saved from death by fire, 58, 59.
,, by the wrong signal, 60-62.
Secret, the, of four letters, or the power of love, 166, 167
Skeleton coming to life illustrating the resurrection, 123, 124

Soldiers, the dying, 90, 91.
Storms, ruled by Christ's kingdom, 56, 57.
Sparrows, God's little girls compared to, 149.
Striker, a, subdued by kindness, 165, 166.
Strong, a little girl made, 218.
Sun, the, works quietly, 165.
„ the, a million times larger than our earth, 53.

Tangles, little, 42.
Tell Jesus, 99.
Thomas, the apostle, a story of, 80, 81.
Tongue, the sand-paper, 173.
Toulouse, the galley-slave, 196–198.
Transfiguration, the, illustrates the resurrection, 126.
Trouble, getting out of, by prayer, 105.
Trust, God's power a ground for, 146.
„ in God, lesson of, taught by shell-fish on the rock, 147.
„ a blind boy's, in his father, 148.
„ perfect, 150.
„ the lost boy's, 152.
„ taught by God's promises, 153.
„ in a promise, 155, 157.
„ in God, only the Christian's privilege, 141.
„ in God, the thought of His promises should lead to, 153.
„ in God, 143.

Voice, a mother's, 168–170.

Walking-stick, sprouting, illustrating the resurrection, 123.
Work, the King's, beauty of, 95, 96.
„ „ the pity in, 96.
Worm, the, in a circle of fire, 213.

www.ingramcontent.com/pod-product-compliance
Lightning Source LLC
Chambersburg PA
CBHW060117170426
43198CB00010B/925